MANAGEMENT AND JOB PERFORMANCE

MANAGEMENT AND JOB PERFORMANCE

ANURADHA SHARMA
Indian Institute of Technology, Delhi
Hauz Khas, New Delhi-110 016

Gian Publishing House
DELHI-110007

First published in 1986

PRINTED IN INDIA

Published by MRS. GAYATRI GARG
for GIAN PUBLISHING HOUSE, Delhi-110 007

Printed by B.N. PRINTERS, Delhi-110 035
at Mohan Printing Corporation, Delhi-110 007

DEDICATED

TO

THE GODDESS OF LEARNING

Preface

THE INTEREST and concern of industrial psychologists, managers and administrators have escalated significantly in the area of work motivation and job performance of employees in recent years. Despite the rapid progress in the field of organizational behaviour, knowledge about human problems in work organizations continues to be the major challenge facing the managers today. Job performance and work motivation of employees is a major re-emerging perspective of management science. This theme of human resources management is in fact the backbone of management philosophy. A philosophy of management which emphasises just on direction and control of employees perhaps is inadequate to motivate them for better performance, in today's context.

Worth of a person and individual differences need to be considered in this regard. The human asset accounting perspective of management gives due importance to such factors. An employee's individual personality make-up and the way of perceiving the work situation are important determinants of his performance. A modest attempt has been made in this study to determine the psychological factors which influence the employees' job performance. This and further researches in this field can provide the managers with an additional tool helpful in selection and placement of personnel and developing various work design strategies.

This book is primarily based on the research work for my Ph.D. thesis and partly on discussions held with a number of Indian managers. In order to make the book both a teaching material and for general reading by interested persons, the ideas have been organized in a fashion that will enable the reader to appreciate the philosophy of organizational behaviour with particular emphasis on job performance. The study reported in this book analyses a number of psychological factors that are related to the level of job performance of the skilled workers in Indian Industrial Organizations. The job performance has been defined as the effectiveness of the workers in terms of productivity and behavioural indices. Based on the pioneering works of Lewin, and Vroom, a cognitive approach to worker's motivation for job performance has been emphasised in this study. Keeping ability a constant factor, job performance has been studied as a result of worker's personality and his perception of the work situation. 397 skilled workers with ITI Diploma were selected for this study. Eight hypotheses have been tested. Results are suggestive of a cognitive organization (i.e. worker's way of viewing the world, his aspirations and values, his perception of the organizational climate), which predicts job performance of the industrial workers.

The book is presented in twelve chapters. Chapters I and II present the introduction, and some related researches. Chapters III IV and V provide an overview and foundation for the reader on the management perspective taken in this book, managerial approaches to work motivation, with some insights from Indian organizations and important theories of work motivations. Chapters VI, VII and VIII deal with the conceptual framework, the hypotheses and the design of the study. An analysis of the concept of job performance and how to measure this has been discussed in Chapter IX. Chapters X and XI present the result of the study, discussion and conclusions. Chapter XII provides a futuristic perspective, looking at the concept of work motivation and job performance in the twenty first century.

My thanks for help in preparing this book go to many people including the managers of various industries with whom I discussed the subject matter to get their views. I am specially thankful to Prof. P. Mathur, Department of Humanities and Social Sciences, IIT Delhi from whom I have learnt much in the course of our close relation as a student and a supervisor. I sincerely thank Prof. B.N. Mukherjee, Indian Statistical Institute, Calcutta, for his kind help and valuable suggestions which I received throughout this study and specially in statistical analyses of the data.

I received help from Dr. J. Kurien of the computer centre of IIT Delhi, the staff of data processing centre of Council for Social Development, New Delhi and Prof. Manek Lal Chaturvedi of the National Council of Educational Research and Training, New Delhi in data processing and in translation of questionnaires into Hindi, respectively. I sincerely thank them.

Managements of all the organizations who permitted me to collect data from their industries, all the employees who participated in this study enthusiatically with co-operative attitudes, and managers who very kindly arranged for my data collection sessions, without whose co-operation my work could not bave completed, deserve special mention. I thank them sincerely.

I am thankful to the Indian Institute of Technology, New Delhi for providing facilities and scholarship to complete my Ph.D. work, on which this book is mainly based.

I hope managers in industries; administrators, researchers in organizational behaviour and teachers in industrial-organizational psychology and management will find this book useful and interesting.

ANURADHA SHARMA

September 9, 1986
198, Sukhdev Vihar,
New Delhi-110025.

Contents

CHAPTER
ONE

Introduction

SUCCESS OF AN ORGANIZATION depends to a great extent upon its people. Peter F. Drucker has recognized the enormous importance of management of people as a resource in his book *The practice of Management*. It is being increasingly realized that the ultimate implementation of management strategies comes through people working in the organization. The fundamental function of management like planning, organizing, decision making, controlling and motivating, all have to be done by people and for people involved in it. This realization has tremendously changed the interpretation of the concept of management in recent years, giving most importance to the management of human resources in various organizations.

Management of Human resources involves several important and complex issues in the form of multi-dimensional reactions involving employee's perception of the organizational climate, personality, background, the objective realities of the organizational culture, leadership styles and intergroup relationship to name a few leading to employee motivation for performance. This concept has changed drastically since the days of Scientific Management. Today the impact of modern behavioural sciences has given new insights and approaches to management of human resources. The management literature has also been greatly enriched by management philosophers, practioners and researchers from behavioural sciences.

This new insight has highlighted the concept of motivating people in organizations, as an important management strategy. Why people are performing well or not doing so has an important motivational component. Motivation for effective work relates to the problems of employees in accomplishing their work. Why different people get motivated on different occasions, what are these factors, are these factors within the individual or in the environment, are some of the questions sought in the theories of work motivation. However, inspite of many theories of work motivation available to us, this still remains a baffling issue and management has always tried to find out the best strategy for motivating people at work.

Thus one of the most important questions facing the industry today is the management of human resources. The prime concern of the managers today is how to motivate employees to get better performance and achieve the goal of the industry. Although managers have always realized that there is some connection between the motivation and employee performance, it is only in recent years that these two concepts have started appearing as twins. The link between these involves a set of highly complex notions about the nature of employees and what motivates them to better job performance leading to greater productivity. In this context, Rush (1969) observed that there is a growing realization that the employee today is, indeed, a new breed. He appears to have different values, different needs and different motivations than his predecessor. He is a product of knowledge explosion. Thus, the earlier meaning of incentives do not seem to work so well. Managing the employee today is an increasingly difficult job. The involvement, sincerity, creativity and dedication to the job that management expects do not seem to be the outcome of financial incentives as was believed earlier. It is observed that inspite of adequate incentives, motivation to better performance is still lacking.

The changing concepts about the management of industrial organizations thus require a new look at the concept of job performance as well. In past, job performance was defined in terms of rise in the level of output of services with the same or reduced level of input as a result of better work methods and improved technology. It is, however, through the employees that the ultimate increase in production is achieved. Their performance is more important than equipment and raw materials. If they are not motivated to work harder, better, with sincerity, initiative and cooperation; no amount of sophisticated technology or improved work method is going to help. Therefore, job performance need to be redefined in terms of employee motivation and satisfaction. Every employee's satisfactory performance is vital to the proper functioning of machinery and equipment in industry, and productivity is more likely to be determined by what the employees rather than machines do.

Every employee has a crystallised and complex sets of needs, values, way of perceiving the world and his personality which he brings with him to his work place. He is, thus, not a raw mould. He tries to fit his psychological make up with the climate of the organization. The fact, that his psychological characteristics influence his behaviour, suggests that his job behaviour and his motivation for job performance will also be influenced by these characteristics. That means, in hiring a worker, one always hires the whole man, and this explains why the improvement of human effectiveness in work is the greatest opportunity for improvement of performance and output of the organization (Drucker 1955).

Managements are trying hard to understand the motivation and job behaviour of the new work force and turning to the field of human behaviour to gain an insight into the problem of job performance. Behavioural science revolution has more recently focussed upon man's needs and values fostering better performance so as to maximise both, human satisfaction and productivity.

In general, productivity of an organization depends upon two major variables, employee job performance and technological factors including equipment, method, job design and raw materials. Disregarding technological considerations, the job performance of the worker depends primarily on employee's ability and motivation to perform. The ability generally depends upon skill, job knowledge and factors like intelligence, but the motivational aspect of the individual job performance is a more complex phenomenon.

According to Gagne and Fleishman (1959), human performance of almost any sort can be improved by increase in motivation. They view that job performance is a function of skill level multiplied by motivation. Vroom (1964) also emphasised that job performance is a result of interaction between worker's skill, ability and motivation.

According to Sutermeister (1963), if a person had no motivation, he could be the most capable individual in the world, but there would be no relationship between his ability and job performance. Thus, both, ability and motivation, are essential aspects of good employee performance. Motivation is considered to result from the interacting forces in physical and social conditions of the job and individual needs. Some forces may act as positive and contribute to motivation, improving job performance of some employees, whereas to others, these may be neutral or even negative reducing employee motivation and resulting in poor performance. What actually happens to employee performance depends on the strength of multitudinous centripetal and contrifugal forces, which may be within the job, within the worker himself or within the organization.

Individual's values, attitudes, habits and beliefs act as a steering system to motivation process affecting the job performance. Work which has become highly complex phenomenon with present technological changes and developments, may be perceived as a task, a duty or an accomplishment, drudgery or even play. It could give intrinsic satisfaction to some and could be drudgery to others. Regardless of its meaning, "work" or "job" cannot be considered apart from the individual who performs it. Therefore, his motives, social interaction and personality must be taken into account to arrive at a conclusion why with the same ability some persons are more effective in the industry than others. Industries have generally overlooked the complexities of human motivation and have tried to oversimplify this by introducing incentives to sustain worker motivation.

Therefore, there is an urgent need to consider this issue, where individual differences play an important role. Under Indian conditions, where we have taken to industrialization in a big way this is a more challenging question. Insights into this problem may help us to develop new design of work and make effective systems. This book is a modest attempt in this direction.

This book is based on a research study of Indian industrial workers. This is an attempt to understand what is lacking in our understanding about employee performance Why there is industrial unrest ? Why some employees just do not want to work ?

Is there a human component which can develop effective human system ? In other words how can we motivate our industrial workers towards better performance ?

The book discusses some theories of work motivation and their applicabilities in the Indian setting. A theoretical model has been proposed which has been tested by a research study. The variables, hypothesis results and analyses of the study have been discussed at the end of the book, when the author tries to analyse the need for understanding new breed of employees and the systems which we are likely to get in the twentyfirst century. This is likely to throw light on the dynamics for better organizatians and effective human systems of future.

The author feels that at the end of this book every reader, whether a researcher, a student, a practitioner or just some one interested in human resources management or human beings would develop some insight into this important problem.

CHAPTER
TWO

Motivation and Job Perfomance : A Research Review

HAWTHORNE STUDIES (Rothlisberger & Dickson 1939) gave important impetus to the study of motivational influences in performance and gave emphasis on supportive organizational relationship and climate as means to boost employee performance. Later, the behavioural theories of management pioneered by Argyris (1957), McGregor (1960) and Likert (1961) focused on motivations implications of job performance. Maslow (1943), Vroom (1964) and Herzberg et al (1959) focused on different aspects of work motivation and job performance. The role of motivational processes in determining worker's job performance is widely recognised by other industrial psychologists as well. Vitles (1953) has identified the "will to work" as industry's core problem in the utilization of its man power resources. Maier (1955) emphasised the need for deeper attention in exploring motivation for better performance in industrial firms. Mehta (1978) on a study to managerial employees and worker representatives has suggested objective and subjective economic factors appear significantly related to life satisfaction and work satisfaction which in turn effects employee's work motivation. The internal motivation appeared to be interacting with organization factors in determing the work motivation.

Konungo (1982) suggested that investigations of organizational phenomenon such as productivity, satisfaction and involvement of worker in their jobs, require some theoretical or rational formulation.

Narain (1973) investigated the factors which influence the motivation and morale of managers in public sector organization. The investigation revealed that the feeling of worthwhile accomplishment and lack or consistenly in management policies were the contributing or intribiting factors in their performance.

Bansal (1982) reported that qualities needed for successful job performance of managers are job knowledge, decision making, good human relations, coordination, leadership, co-operation, communication, need for power, need for occupational achievement and intelligence.

Rajappa (1978) has highlighted the importance of working environment in the analysis of work motivation. Results of his study reveal that organizations with achievement oriented climate were highly productive organizations. Sharma (1983) has also emphasised the importance of organizational climate in employee work motivation. Based on a survey of fifty industrial organizations in India, he observed that grievance handling, recognition and appreciation, participative Management and scope far advancement are inportant factors in an organizational climate enhancing work motivation of employees. In other words what is required is the improvement of quality of work life and not merely the material benefits.

Singh and Singh (1982) studied the relationship of ego strength participation and job anxiety to the productivity/performance of six hundred blue collar workers. Results of the investigation reveal that productivity of individuals is not only associated with physical environment of work but it has definite relationship with psychological variables also.

In another study Singh and Singh (1982) reported that participation and job anxiety play an important role in determining the level of performance of blue collar workers, this study was conducted in a textile firm, with a sample of 150 workers, in India.

Pestonjee and Singh (1982) in a study of 600 rank and file workers of a textile unit in India suggested that anxiety and job involvement have significant impact on performance. Anxiety was found to be detrimental to performance.

Lal and Bhardwajs' (1981) study has brought out important

fact that no organizational policy for improving morale, motivation and performance of the workers can be equally effective for all levels of workers, hence motivational strategies need a careful consideration.

In another study Mehta (1978) discussed the problem of employee work motivation as an organization development strategy. According to his analysis there lies the crucial need for motivating and promoting greater human satisfaction in organizations in order to achieve the desired organizational objectives and higher productivity.

Gupta, Pestonjee and Singh (1982) armed at studying the relationship of alienation, participation and anxiety to worker efficiency. Based on a questionnaire survey, a study was conducted on twenty five workers of a file manufacturing unit in India. The findings suggest that the knowledge of the level of efficiency may act as a moderator between alienation efficiency and participation efficiency relationships.

Bhushan Lal (1984) in a study of library personnel reported that certain psychological variables like fulfilment of security, social and esteem needs, internality in locus of control, job satisfaction and job involvement are significant contributors of job performance.

Sinha (1973) studied 811 managers at three levels from two steel and two coal industries from public and private sector organizations in India. Results of the study reveal that Managers of public sector firms had an unfavourable overall image of the organization.

England, Dhingra and Aggrawal (1974) studied the relationship between job success and job value. They have reported a correlation of .35 between these two variables.

Bose (1976) studied the relationship between organizational stress and managerial performance. The sample consisted of 59 managers at three levels in a large business organization. The study reveals that the performance score of upper level managers correlated significantly with organizational strees scorss.

Mathur and Sharma (1978) reported that the job performance of skilled workers in industries seems to be related to the attitudes towards working climate, particularly those giving satisfaction to higher order needs in Maslow's need hierarchy theory.

Dwivedi (1980) studied the relationship, between background

variables, attitudes, pay and employee performance. This study on 62 employees from a printing press revealed that there was significant positive correlation between performance and attitude towards supervisor and pay. In another study Dwivedi (1978) investigated the relationship between personality characteristics, as measured by MMPI, and supervisory performance. It was found that correlation between some scores on subscales of MMPI and the performance was positive.

Sharma and Mathur (1982) reported that the correlates of job satisfaction and job performance are not the same. Therefore a simplistic assumption that a satisfied employee is the better performer will not be very appropriate. Perhaps we need to study the dynamics of this relationship more deeply.

Sharma and Mathur (1981) investigated the relationship between employee's values and their job performance. The analysis revealed that some values are positively related to job performance of industrial workers.

Sharma and Mathur (1981) analysed the relationship between employees' socio-economic status and their job behaviour. There seems to be a positive relationship between the two variables.

Several earlier studies reported in India and other countries also stressed on the role different motivating factors in employee job performance. Bose (1956) emphasised the role of machine efficiency as limited by human factors. He viewed that, for attaining maximum productivity, worker has to be motivated apart from his training and experience. Singh and Baumgartel (1966) studied the job related to need of blue and white collar workers and airline mechanics in India. They found the needs for advancement and security and level of educational achievement bearing a positive relationship with performance.

Mukherjee (1968) has made some inferences regarding the prepotency of job-related needs of factory workers employed in a progressive textile mill. Results clearly supported the hypothesis that hygiene factors in general are ranked higher than motivators.

Ganguly (1954) in a study of 380 workers in an Indian Engineering Industry in Calcutta concluded that Indian workers desire a steady job, an adequate income, opportunity for learning new trades, status and increased social approval. These factors are motivators for better job performance. Katz, Maccoby and Morse (1950); and Katz, Maccoby, Gurin and Floor (1951) did not find any difference between high and low producing groups regarding satisfaction with wages and job status. Likert (1961) has suggested that relationship between satisfaction and performance becomes more positive as the level of skill required by the job increases. Fleishman (1958) experimentally manipulated the motivation and found that performance was significanlty higher under high motivation condition than under low. Vroom (1959) examined the correlation between scores on four tests of ability and four measures of job performance in case of industrial workers who were classified under high, moderator and low motivation for effective performance. He found fairly high positive correlation between ability and performance of employees in high motivation group. Similar results were reported by French (1957).

UNESCO (1961) study in two regions in India near Bombay and Calcutta reported positive relationship between attitude towards management and employee productivity.

Bose (1958) concluded that the productivity is definitely influenced by some psychological factors like, attitudes and job satisfaction.

Brayfield and Crocket (1955) found that there was little evidence of any simple or appreciable relationship between employee attitude and his performance. Katzell Barret and Parker (1961) however, have shown that some kind of objective criterion of job performance shows relationship with satisfcation measures.

The fact, that personality factors and socio-cultural milieu moderate the influence on job performance, has generally been overlooked. Some of the studies by Vroom (1960) and Stephen (1966) have, however, focused on these fields.

Mukherjee and Menon (1969) examined the effect of an incentive scheme in operation in moulding section of a plastic industry, and relationship between output rates and certain psychological aspects of the worker such as his anxiety, conflict, etc. These authors concluded that there exists no relationship between productivity trend and these personality characteristics.

Sinha (1966) observed that individual cases of behavioral difficulties crop up every now and then and a considerable amount of management's resources are spent annually because of labour turnover and replacement of emotionally maladjusted workers. This has serious repercussions on the employers. Veeraraghavan (1962) aimed at understanding the socio-economic and personality differences among workers and their attitude towards supervision.

Ganguly (1953) studied the relationships between intelligence, age, education, pay, personality traits and worker's attitude towards management, and has concluded that management should take care to apply right type of incentive which will create interest among workers and foster on them a feeling of identification with the organization.

The influence of supervision on job performance of work groups has been reported by Davis (1962) and Likert (1959). They concluded that 'employee oriented' supervisors tend to get better productivity.

Bose (1957), Sequeira (1962), James and Kanungo (1966) have also emphasised the importance of the type of supervision on employee job performance. Bose (1955) concluded that employee centered supervision was positivley correlated to productivity and morale.

Schein (1970) has also stressed upon the social nature of man and has viewed it as a primary dominant factor in determining the job performance.

Pestonjee and Akhtar (1969) studied the relative significance of ten intrinsic factors in motivating workers. Advancement, participation and recognition were rated more important than pay in their study. Similar results are reported by Akhtar and Pestonjee (1969) in another study. Thanga (1959) analysed the effect of the level of aspirating employees in a telephone factory. Bhatt's (1962) study revealed that out of the nine possible incentives, choice of work and advancement were most preferred ones. Benefits, working conditions and supervision were reported to be less important motivating factors in their investigation.

Ganguly (1961) emphasised that employee productivity is a function of the number and strength of needs that must be satisfied through high production, the degree of probability that high productivity will satisfy these needs and the amount of increase in productivity that will be required to satisfy these needs. Thus he stressed upon need fulfilment and expectancy as related to employee productivity.

Pervin (1968) treated performance as a function of the interaction between the characteristics of the individual and those of the environment.

Feather (1961) and Forhand and Gilmer (1964) discussed the

interactions between personalities and job qualities leading to high efficiency.

Allen (1973) has proposed a theory 'M' for management. On the basis of a survey of the opinions of 259 managers, he concluded that behaviour is influenced by complex psychological, biological, social and economic factors. Most people tend to be concerned with their own needs and objectives. Often, right action is blocked by characteristics of their personalities and circumstances beyond their control. Some people lack contribution and dislike responsibility, some are just the opposite, but majority falls in between. Allen does not agree with the idea that happy and satisfied employees are better in job performance.

In the light of his data, Allen proposes a new theory called 'theory M' and views that people are motivated to work by highly complex factors as stated earlier. Personalities, their early upbringing and circumstances often prevent the workers in doing what is right. An average man is by nature primarily concerned with his own needs as he sees them. There is individual difference in assuming responsibility, and ambition. Managers are as human as those they manage. Real progress will occur when both supervisors and subordinates try to understand the needs and roles of the other and develop better ways of achieving common objectives. According to theory M, then, a mix of good pay and social satisfaction is more important than either by itself, and will be a responsible factor for better job performance.

Choudhury (1955), attempted to study the issue of worker's participation problem in India. She concluded that the best way of tapping the human factor is through worker's participation in problems related to efficiency. Billimoria's (1960) study also supported this view. Sreeniwasan (1964) studied the relationship between worker's social environment and productivity. Sinha and Gupta (1974) indicated that higher the need satisfaction, the more regular was the worker at the job.

Hunt (1963) stressed that interactions among modes of response, situations and persons were more inportant in behaviour than any of the individual sources of variance alone. Rausch, Dittman and Taylor (1959) have presented a study on the interaction between personality characteristics and environmental conditions in predicting porformance.

Inspite of various studies on job performance and its correlates, some gaps still remain, specially in Indian context. Conditions under which job attitudes will affect job performance are not clearly discernible from the researches. Worker's need satisfaction perception and his personality may jointly determine his level of job performance. These factors, when studied jointly may throw more light on the dynamics of job performance. Sharma (1973) has emphasised that much remains to be done to study the effect of deprivation of social esteem and self-actualization needs of the workers as related to their accomplishment at the jobs. He further points out that specially lacking are the studies investigating the relationship between attitude, job satisfaction and productivity. The effects of formal organizations as related to worker's productivity has also been a relatively unexplored area (Sinha 1972). Further, few studies have tried to analyse personality of the workers in this context. These studies have reflected the problem as a complex one, which can be better conceptualised in terms of a psychological contract entered into by both, worker and organization, resulting in better job performance. For an individual worker, both, intrinsic and extrinsic factors may determine his level of job performance. The present investigation is a modest attempt to fill these research gaps. The aim here is to study the relationships of different background variables, personality variables and perception of need satisfaction in terms of attitudes of the skilled workers in some public and private industrial organizations in India, to job performance. These motivating factors in the job situation, job itself and within the worker himself may jointly determine the job performance and throw light on intrinsic and extrinsic factors in worker's motivation.

CHAPTER
THREE

Management Perspective

SINCE THIS BOOK is about management and employee performance, a brief note on aspects of management seems necessary.

Management is often defined as controlling, planning, directing and motivating. Here the emphasis is only on motivating. This is not overlooking the importance of other aspects of management, but trying to put forward an indepth understanding of employee performance in motivational perspective.

Therefore, the interface with other management strategies like planning, technical appraisals, time budgeting, financial budgeting operations research and industrial relations are not the central cencern here. The focal point here is the human asset accounting. Human asset or resource accounting are slowly beginning to have an effect. This concept formally recognizes the monetary value of a human being in organization. If a good employee leaves the organization, the organization is at a loss not only because of the replacement cost but because of his individual worth. Likert (1967) suggests that level of intelligence, aptitude, quality of decision making, communication and control are some of the important variables in this context. Behaviourally oriented approach to employee performance suggested in this study is thus important in human asset accounting idea.

Management may like to take the macro approach to industrial productivity, where over all organizational effectiveness is the concern (it could also be at much larger plane like national level). Some organizations prefer to analyse the performance at sub unit level or departmental level. However, here the emphasis is placed on individual employee's performance; a micro analytic approach.

CHAPTER
FOUR

Managerial Approaches to Work Motivation

MANAGERIAL APPROACHES have evolved alongwith the development of organizations at different times. Management philosophy initially developed with scientific management philosophy and human relations approach. The recent emphasis, however, is on the human potential and human resources approach. It is neither easy nor right to say, which one is the best approach, perhaps effective management may require the right combination of the components of these approaches. In Indian Management style also one finds a combination of scientific management principle and human relations approach, with little emphasis on human resources approach. These approaches are discussed in this chapter alongwith a case study analysis of few Indian Industries.

SCIENTIFIC MANAGEMENT

Until the later part of the nineteenth century, not much attention was paid to human factors in their contribution industries. Workers were more or less treated like commodities, the idea that workers were like something that could be brought and only little attention was to be paid to them as individuals was the only way of managing an industry. Around the same time Taylor (1911) pioneered the "scientific management" movement. This movement aimed at systematising managerial practices. He stressed on the need for standardization and control in operation of firms. Scientific management combines a study of physical capabilities of a worker (as is still done by industrial engineers in time and motion studies) coupled with an economic incentive approach. The central idea of the approach has been that, if material rewards are closely related to work efforts, the worker will respond with the maximum standard of job performance, he is physically capable of. Although Taylor originally started his study on the interaction between human characteristics and the characteristics of machine, the two elements which are major constituents of the industrial work process, he ended up by focusing on the physical characteristics of the human body in routine jobs. Taylor overlooked the social and psychological aspects of the job and the satisfaction a worker must get at work.

HUMAN RELATIONS APPROACH

In the early scientific management movement, the employee was seen as primarily motivated by economic incentives. The managerial approach in industries took a turn and the most significant event which brought about a different view was the Hawthorne Studies (Mayo 1933), Rothlisberger and Dickson (1939). From their studies emerged the idea that there is a relationship between productivity and attitudes of the employees. Mayo and his associates emphasised that a factory was a social system in itself, and group dynamics in the work situation had a vital role to play in industrial management. The industrial worker was then viewed as a human being with his attitudes, values, wants and desires influencing his effectiveness in the organization. They emphasised that the amount of work carried out by a worker is not only determined by his physical capacity, as proposed by scientific management, but also by social factors. They also stressed on the importance of non-economic rewards in determining the motivation and happiness of workers. They also argued that the narrow specialisation is by no means the most efficient form of division of labour. They viewed that workers do not react to management and its norms and individual rewards, so much, as they do as group members. Thus the role of communication, participation and leadership are important factors in industrial management.

Inspite of certain criticism on the methods of study used by Mayo and his associates, Hawthorne studies proved to be a landmark in ensuring human relations movement. Numerous studies to the aid of industrial world are being conducted by social scientists and surely this movement has crystallized into a body of knowledge in management of human resources. This approach has marked the origin of school though with emphasis on social concepts that have been useful in understanding the dynamics of human behaviour in organisations. These studies have uncovered the importance of social incentives in the workplace. They stress on the importance of human elements and social factors, contributing to productivity.

The human relations movement in industry emphasised on creating work force with high morale and represented an attempt to breakdown formal boundaries that are part of the bureaucratic organisation structure.

According to Knowles (1958), the human relations approach to the problems of industry asserts that some combinations of personalities, groups and organisations produce conflict, frustration and mental illness, and that other combinations produce harmony satisfaction and mental health. The approach recognised that the human beings acquire definite attitudes. Thus, this is a tremendous contribution to industrial management science.

With the acceptance and importance of human relations movement, increasing emphasis has also been given to the worker as a whole man. No longer a worker is regarded solely as an economic tool. He is driven and controlled by diverse factors of environment and has expectations, desires and values. How he performs on his job depends on this total make up of personality to a great extent.

HUMAN RESOURCES APPROACH

Organizational behaviour is a system consisting of the interacting elements of formal organization and human beings. Individual interacts with this formal organization to satisfy his needs that impinge on his total personality. Consequently the behavioural outcomes in the organization reflect as much the dynamics of the organization as the modification of individual's behaviour in terms of need satisfaction.

A given work situation has three important aspects, i.e. structure of its own, its own processes of communication and decision making, and application of certain techniques or knowledge to work. In the process of interaction with the work situation, the individual tries to satisfy his needs involving his own personality. Consequently, it is a question of the change the individual undergoes to modify his behaviour in the organization. Thus, the total output of his behaviour is a function of the inputs that the formal organization provides him with, and the pattern of psychological processes that work within him. With the growth of the human relations movement, increasing emphasis has been given to the worker as a whole man. No longer is he viewed solely as an economic tool, but as a human being, who is driven and controlled by diverse elements of society and has fears, frustrations, desires, values, and expectations which affect his total personality. How he performs on his job, i.e. his efficiency and productivity, are dependent as much, if not more, on the external aspects surrounding his work place, as on the tools and materials he uses. Therefore, it must be recognised that man as a worker is unique compared to other resources of the organization. He must be motivated not only to do his job but to strive constantly to improve his performance. This then, remains the cardinal objective of the human relations functions to discover the newer and better ways of understanding man and his work behaviour so as to help people to realize their maximum potential.

In recent years assumption of human relations approach have been challenged by a number of researchers like McGregar (1960), Argyris (1957), Schein (1972) and Likert (1967) etc., who have highlighted the human resources approach. This is not an oversimplified approach like human relations approach. This views that human beings are motivated by a complex set of interrelated factors. These factors take into account the enormous talent, and potential an individual brings to his work place with him. It is a question of giving him opportunities to utilize his talent. creativity and potentials by giving him a meaningful work assignment and by adding greater responsibility, autonomy, variety etc. It may be interesting to know more about theories of Argyris and McGregor which are important contributions in this regard.

THEORY 'X' AND THEORY 'Y'

According to McGregor (1960), traditional organization with its centralised decision making, superior subordinate pyramid and external control of work is based upon assumption about human nature and motivation. He proposed two theories about human behaviour and motivation. These are theory 'X' and theory 'Y'. Theory 'X' assumes that most people prefer to be directed, are lazy, cannot assume responsibility and want safety above all. This theory believes that money, fringe benefits and threat of punishment are the motivators. After describing this theory, McGregor questioned whether this view is correct in the present industrial context. Drawing heavily on Maslow's hierarchy of needs (presented in the next chapter) McGregor concluded that assumptions of theory 'X' about nature of man are generally inaccurate, and management cannot reach its goal if this philosophy is followed. McGregor suggested that better understanding of human nature and motivation are necessary for better management.

He developed an alternative theory called theory 'Y'. According to this theory, people are not to be considered lazy and unreliable by nature. In this theory he said that man can be basically self directed and creative at work if properly motivated. Therefore, it should be an essential task of the management to realise the potential of man. The motivated worker can achieve his own goals. Theory 'Y' further assumes that motivation occurs at the social, esteem and selfactualization levels as well as at the security level (Please refer to Maslow's theory in the next chapter). However, employees are able to achieve the satisfaction of these needs in very few organizations. Often organizations do not pay attention to these need satisfactions. Further, McGregor feels that work can be as natural and satisfying as play. Unfortunately such is the case with only few organizations, where cohesive work groups have developed, and people come to work gladly because work is inherently satisfying to them.

ARGYRIS'S THEORY

The impact of organisation on worker's job performance and motivation has been highlighted in Argyris's (1957) theory. He examined the industrial organisations to determine the effect of management practices on personal growth and individual behaviour within the work environment. According to this theory the management has to provide a work climate in which every worker has an opportunity to grow psychologically. An individual-satisfying his own needs while working for the success of the organizations. If the work environment does not provide for such growth opportunities people may get frustration, maladjustment and this will adversely affect the output. Most of the organizations by their very nature may do some damage to the individual. The main point is that few managers understand and recognise the social and psychological effects of their policies. According to him, the value system of bureaucracy itself has to be modified before individual growth and productivity can be attained (Argyris 1957, 1962). He argues that bureaucratic values, which dominate organization life, are basically impersonal values. These values lead to non-authentic relationship between organisation and its members, which in turn decreases the organizational effectiveness. The values which permit and reinforce the expression of feelings are the norm of individuality and trust which may contribute to better effectiveness of the workers. The theory emphasises that industrial organizations, as they have been traditionally run, are just out of match with the normal needs of a mature adult. Thus, Argyris's point of focus is the individual himself, who arrives at the industry as a matured person but whose emotional maturity, i.e. his realism can vary from highly developed to childish. How a situation would affect a given worker depends on how mature he is. Argyris further says that the main mechanism through which an organization frustrates the mature employee and encourages the immature one to stay, are the formal organization structure, directive leadership, and managerial controls. The effect of these mechanism is different on different people as they significantly differ in their needs and aspirations. The concentration of decision making power in a few hands may be detrimental to the mental health of the workers in industry and may affect the output of the workers.

MANAGERIAL APPROACHES IN INDIAN ORGANIZATIONS

Indian industries have also been using different management

strategies for motivating their workers for better performance. However, as it is true of many other countries, because of different organizational set-ups and ownerships management of human resources show different patterns. Much depends on the philosophy and the culture of the organization which flows from what the owner or top person wants to do. There are a number of organizations where bureaucatic values are there and are quite important. There are few smaller organizations, generally in the private sector, where the climate is participate—democratic. There are organizations trying to change themselves to participative organizations. Motivation for work is considered important in every organization. However, the strategies are different. The most common being the money as a motivator. However, money factor combined with some self esteem and social factors have achieved better results. Few case studies are presented here which may highlight the managerial approaches to work motivation in India to some extent.

Case I

Organization is a public limited company, producing a consumer item, with about 2000 employees. The wage/salary structure is one of the best in the country and bonus is one of highest paid amount. This is an assembly line organization. Within the plant the physical working conditions are rather difficult (because of the temperature, fumes etc.). However, the organization maintains a good relationship with union leaders and productivity is a joint effort. Motivation of workers is sustained through investing like some short trips to a hill station on weekends at the subsidised rates, organizing fete and presentations at Diwali festival. There is individual incentive scheme too. There are hardly any reports of strikes in their organization. The company runs extremely well and people seem to be happy too. The organization thus appreciates the scientific managemant approach, coupled with human relations approach.

Case II

This is a small scale engineering industry. The Industry is new and has just started establishing and stabilizing itself. The owner of the industry is a highly qualified postgraduate dynamic, intelligent engineer. This person is very sincere, honest and straight forward by nature and wanted to inculcate such values in his workers also. However, with a struggle of few years he finds that he has to be the part of the total industrial climate and the important factor for motivating workers at the lower level of employment is money. If money is just little over the prevailing market rate combined with opportunity of increasing technical calibre (which this industry provides much more than larger organizations) the motivation of the workers can be sustained. Further when workers are sent out on duty (on site) for a short time, they seem to enjoy the work more and get more involved. This top person has created participative climate at the shop floor level, where most of the manufacturing ideas and problems are discussed. Rarely has any one been fired (even for a mistake resulting into a financial loss to the organization). The organization) however, doesn't make huge profits. Keeping money factor constant, the industry, thus applies the human resources approach to management and work motivation.

Case III

This is a public sector organization. The unit had the major problem of industrial relations and strikes. The motivation and incentive systems are just the same as in any other public sector organization in India. However, a change in the managerial strategies with participative management brought great improvement in the system. Instead of confronting and firing the union leaders. they were sent to Japan to see the Japanese system of work culture. This tremendously improved their sense of commitment, involement and motivation work. Being the leaders of workers they also tried to propagate these ideas at the workers levels. Thus the industry runs with participative style of management, with good pay structure as well.

Case IV

This is a case study of a small scale industry, with sophisticated tool room facility, manufacturing a precision engineering item. The proprietor of the firm, though a technically qualified person has not been able to run his industry very successfully because he pays average, the working climate is average, and opportunities for learning and development are just nil. Therefore the worker output is also not very high and worker turnover is too high. In this case perhaps no specific management philosophy is followed.

By analysing the different types of organizations in India. One can see that though the strategies and philosophies are different in big and the small organizations, one thing comes out to be important, that psycho-social factors are important elements of work motivation system and every individual should be paid due attention, growth opportunity, incentive, and a fairdeal. However, it is important to mention that we need a managerial strategy which is Indian, in the sense which matches with our cultural norms, climatic conditions and psycho-socio-economic factors. This change is inevitable like change in dress or architecture. In this context it becomes important to analyse what is important factor in work motivation of workers, i.e. looking at the problem from worker's point of view. The next section of this book discusses some theories of work motivation and an analysis, based on some interviews from workers. However, further chapters dealing with a main study also try to analyse the factors related to work motivation of industrial workers.

CHAPTER
FIVE

Theories of Work Motivations

WHENEVER I have had the opportunity to interact with executives in organizations, the most commonly asked and discussed behavioural science technique is about how can one increase the work motivation of employees at various levels. The techniques, most of the managers have been using are the traditional tools of reward and punishment. If the dynamics of work motivation would have been as simple as that, i.e. punishing for mistakes and rewarding for success we would have solved most of the job performance problems by now. The problem is that motivation to work, like any other motivational situation, is a highly complex phenomenon. The impact of reward and punishment can be generalized only on a very broad level. These extrinsic factors seem to work through the intrinsic psychological states. For example money as a motivator has a number of theoretical explanations. It could be a reinforcing event for one employee and would be recognition for another person, yet another employee may consider this as an anxiety reducing security factor. Whereas this could be achievement for another group of persons. Therefore translating these behavioural science researches into management techniques is an important aspect and perhaps a hard won skill. Every Manager and researcher in the area of the analysis of job performance will perhaps be benefited by some theories of work motivation, which have been proposed, tested and applied in organizations.

Here three theories of work motivations in industrial organizations are discussed. Some research reviews related to these theories from Indian and other countries are also presented. These are the theories proposed by Maslow, Herzberg et. al. and Vroom. This is not to say that these are the only theories analysing work motivation, but these most popular theories form the basis of a research study, which is reported in this book.

MASLOW'S THEORY OF NEED HEIRARCHY

One of the popular theories of human motivation formulated by Maslow (1943) is based on the propositions that needs are important. These needs are arranged in a heirarchy of importance (ranging from the lowest to the highest, i.e. from physiological, to safety then social and love needs, need for self esteem and finally to self actualization need) and that the most urgent need will monopolise the individual attention while less prepotent needs are minimised for the moment. All needs are never fully satisfied. As soon as one need is satisfied it is replaced by a higher need. Thus, once a need is fairly well satisfied, it no longer motivates employee behaviour and next higher need becomes the motivator, but any time if lower need is threatened, the pattern may reverse and that need can become the motivator. These needs are interdependent and overlapping. Fig 1 shows the heirarchy of needs.

Included in the physiological need category are needs for food, water, air, sleep, and sex etc. Safety needs are expressed as desires for protection against danger and deprivation. Since every industrial employee is at least partially dependent in his employer, safety needs are expressed as a desire for security, which may also take the form of quests for job security and economic security. Social needs include the feeling of belongingness, association, love and acceptance. These become major motivating factors when the other lower needs are fairly well satisfied. Esteem needs refer to the satisfaction of ego needs. Generally it has been observed that the typical industrial organization, offers only limited opportunities for the satisfaction of these needs specially at the lower level of employment. Self esteem needs include self confidence, self respect, competence, achievement, independence, freedom, status appreciation, recognition etc. The self actualization need comes only after all other needs have been satisfied reasonably. Self actualization

Maslow's need heirarchy and its interpretation as a heirarchy of factors related to work motivation

Self actualization needs
(Realising one's inner potentials)

Esteem needs
(Status symbols, promotions appreciations and awards.)

Social and belongingness needs
(Affiliation needs through formal and informal groups in organizations)

Sefty and Security needs
(Seniority, job security, unions, money etc.)

Physiological needs
(Basic needs like food, shelter which perhaps pay can provide to some extent)

Fig. 1

needs include the realization of one's potentials, creativity in the broadest sense and self development etc. Maslow (1954) expressed it as "what a man can be, he must be." He emphasized that the theory is primarily a framework for future research.

Porter (1966) provides empirical data concerning Maslow's model. He has tried to measure all but physiological needs on a sample covering different managerial levels in a wide range of business organizations in the United States and thirteen other countries. His findings point out that regardless of country or managerial level, higher the need in hierarchy, less it is satisfied. Beer (1966) found that workers (female clerks) when asked to arrange their needs in a hierarchy by ranking method, tend to arrange them as predicted by Maslow. He also reported that self actualization, autonomy and social needs are most important. Beer concluded that the model has little usefulness for a theory of industrial motivation, although it may provide a fairly reliable measurement of the needs of the industrial workers.

Lawler and Porter (1967) correlated satisfaction of managers needs with their performance. All correlations were significant but low. Lawler and Porter conclude that satisfaction of higher order needs in more closely related to performance than satisfaction of lower order needs.

In a study hypothesising work behaviour, Korman (1970) points out that this theoretical approach has gained great popularity in many management and psychological circles, but one wonders why it has been tested only once as a theory of performance in Industrial context and that too it provided little or no support to the theory. In Indian settings also a number of studies have been reported which have tried to test Maslow's model. Some of the studies conducted in the industrial context are reported here.

Research results related to Maslow's Theory from India

Mathur and Sharma (1978) and Sharma (1977) tried to analyse need related employee attitudes and their relationship to job performance. In a study of industrial skilled workers they reported that Maslow's higher order needs perceived by them is related to their job satisfaction and to some extent with job performance. Sinha and Gupta (1974) studied need satisfaction of industrial workers from a glass manufacturing company. Findings show that the average need satisfaction score for lower order needs was much lower than social and esteem needs. The study shows that needs are not arranged in the hierarchical order as suggested by Maslow.

Singhal (1974, 1975, 1976) studied the perceptual gap in need gratification of industrial employees, need importance and need gratification and problems of absenteeism in relation to need satisfaction. Results are similar on all these studies. Least perceptual gap was reported on safety needs and large gaps on physiological, and self actualization needs. These studies also show that workers at different levels differ significantly in their need importance. Perhaps needs cannot be placed in hierarchy as suggested by Maslow.

Study by Gupta (1977) on three hundred working women from four professions support the need heirarchy model of Maslow. In a study of one hundred and seventy seven government executives, Agrawal and Sharma (1977) reported little support for the need of hierarchy. The study reveals that the needs do not follow ascending order, but almost a descending pattern. They further suggested that needs follow a spiral pattern rather than a ladder pattern. Ravikumar and Harigopal (1978) in a study of managerial personnel, using porter's need satisfaction questionnaire reported that lower order needs are less important than the higher order needs.

Srivastava (1978) reported on the basis of his study of executives that lower level executives are more bothered about the basic needs, whereas higher level executives are more concerned with higher order needs.

This research review reveals that except one or two studies, most of the studies donot support the need hierarchy pattern. Perhaps every person arranges hierarchy according to his priority.

HERZBERG'S MOTIVATION HYGIENE THEORY

The theory of work motivation advanced by Frederic Herzberg and his associates (1959) has been referred to as Motivation hygiene theory. This is based on data collected from 200 Pittsburgh accountants and engineers. They used semistructured interviews to find out the experience at work, which resulted in either a marked improvement or marked reduction in their job satisfaction. They also studied how this feeling of job satisfaction affected their work performance. Content analysis of the interviews suggested that certain job characteristics led to job satisfaction, while a different set of job characteristics led to dissatisfaction. The satisfiers relate to the content or nature of the job. The factors that lead to satisfaction include achievement, recognition, intrinsic characteristic of the job itself, responsibility and advancement. Poor working conditions led to dissatisfaction, but good working conditions did not necessarily lead to satisfaction. This shows that these two are not simple opposites. Hence, a two-factor theory of motivation was proposed. Fig. 2 presents these points.

Herzberg's Motivation—Hygiene Theory

Hygiene Factors		*Motivators*
Company Policy Administration Working conditions Wages/Salary Supervision Inter presonal relations		Variety Growth opportunity Responsibility Recognition Work itself

Fig. 2

Job content characteristics were called "Motivators" by Herzberg and his co-workers. According to them they satisfied the individuals need for self actualization at work. The job environment characteristics which led to dissatisfaction, were called

"Hygienes" because they were work supporting or contextual rather than task-determined. Thus, motivators include achievement, recognition, advancement, possibility, and work itself. Hygienes include salary, supervision, company policy, administration, job security, working conditions etc. As hygienes remove health hazards, it is preventive rather than curative, hygiene factors also have similar impact on employee motivation. Herzberg contends that only the satisfiers are motivators and dissatisfiers are maintenance factors, because their presence is needed to maintain a person's level of performance i.e. more of this will not add to performance but less will lower it.

Empirical evidence for this theory includes that of Herzberg's himself. However, it was found that all the studies using the critical incidence technique confirm the theory. Whereas those using other methods give less favourable results. House and Wigdor (1967), Hulin and Smith (1967), Lindsay, Marks and Gorlow (1967).

Dunnettee, Cambell and Hakel (1967) concluded that achievements, recognition and responsibility seem important for both, satisfaction and dissatisfaction, whereas such dimensions as security, salary and working conditions are less important. They further commented that, if the data are analysed in terms of percentage differences and in terms of ranks, the results are different. Reynold (1973) proposed that the perceptual defence illustrated by Herzberg's studies can provide the basis for an alternative explanation of commitment to work.

Khan (1961) points out that it is likely that an individual needs to feel he is competent. 'Recognition' then means that his competence is appreciated. 'Unfairness', which appears at the opposite end of the scale to "recognition", is by way of focusing the attention on the lapse of others in appreciation of his worth.

Some Indian Studies

Lahiri and Srivastava (1967) contrast two job factors to illustrate, that individuals attributed dissatisfaction to environmental factors rather than to self.

Rao (1973), and Rao and Rao (1973) reported studies in which two factor theory could not receive unequivocal support. It was observed that motivators contributed to both, satisfied and dissatisfied feelings. Motivator and hygiene factors were found not to be mutually exclusive in the factor analytic sense.

Dayal and Saiyadin (1970) reported that their findings are highly supportive of Herzberg's Motivation-hygiene theory. They concluded that the findings are all the more meaningful in view of the cross cultural differences pointing towards universality of human motivation.

Inspite of large number of studies criticising Herzberg's motivation-hygiene theory it is still significant as it separates motivation from hygiene factor which has led to the theory of 'job enrichment.'

While there are some similarities between Maslow's need hierarch and Herzberg's model, there are differences as well. According to Maslow, any need can be a motivator, if it is relatively less satisfied, however, Herzberg views only higher order needs as the motivators.

Considering the model of Herzberg and Maslow to the accomplishment of organisational objective, there is need to translate the findings into usable motivational strategies and recommend incentives for promoting such objectives as better job performance. There seems to be little evidence empirically relating Maslow's theory to job performance. Although Herzberg asked his respondents to report the effect of job events on their performance, only two studies which attempt to measure performance independent of respondents response have been reported where performance seems to be influenced by motivators that are present in the job.

Hunt and Hill (1969) emphasize that neither of these theories handle the problem of individual differences in motivation.

VROOM'S MODEL OF MOTIVATION FOR JOB PERFORMANCE

Vroom (1964) looks at effective motivation not in terms of either a fixed set of human needs or as a uniform configuration of external motivations. He defines motivation as a process governing the choices, made by the persons among alternative forms of volunatary activity. Thus, motivation is a result of goals that a person wants to achieve. These goals may be different for different persons. These might be higher salary, promotion and job security, for some and more interesting work for others. The emphasis, is on what goal the employee sees as important. Therefore the major factor affecting employee productivity is the relationship a person perceives between productivity and personal goal attainment. If an employee believes that there is little or nothing he can do to influence his performance, his attempts to do the job may be weak. It is the perception of ability to affect his productivity that counts. This model suggests likelihood of differences in motivational states among different persons.

Vroom has proposed two models of his instrumentality or expectancy theory. One deals with the prediction of the anticipated satisfaction associated with something individual wants to attain (outcome) rather than the actual satisfaction attained. This model is often applied to the prediction of "job satisfaction". An individual's satisfaction with his job is assumed to be a function of the degree to which he sees the job as leading to other outcomes and anticipated satisfactions (Fig. 3).

Vroom's Theory of Work Motivation

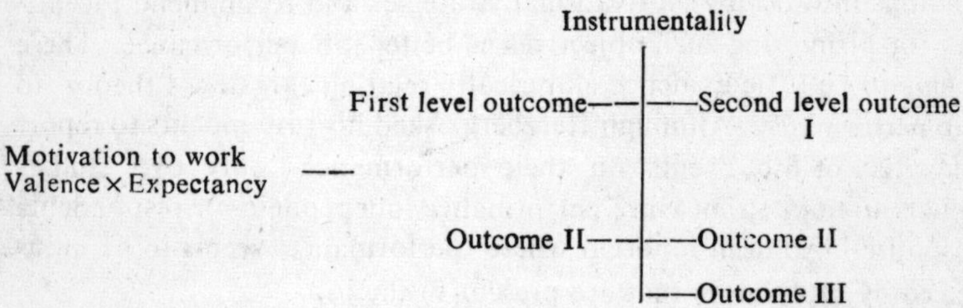

Fig. 3

The second model of Vroom (1964) predicts 'job performance', predicting the amount of effort or behaviour required to accomplish a task goal. The major difference between the two models is that instrumentalities are perceived as correlation between outcome in the satisfaction model, while in the job performance model, expectancies are perceived as probabilities of outcomes of certain actions (Shrode and Voich 1974). Two concepts are introduced to explain the method of determining preferences for outcomes. These are 'valence' and 'instrumentality'. Valence refers to the strength of an individual's perception of the relationship between a first level outcome and second level outcomes. Important goals of industrial workers often cited in empirical literature are promotion, pay, pleasant working conditions and job security. In addition to this, each worker can be asked to indicate the likelihood of a certain job behaviour, such as, the high productivity will lead to any of the goals described. Vroom expresses the valence of a first level outcome of a person as a monotonically increasing function of an algebraic sum of the products of the valences of the (second level) outcomes.

If an individual desires promotion and feels that superior performance is very strong factor in achieving that goal, his first level outcomes are levels of performance and second level outcome is promotion. In Vroom's term, performance varies directly with the product of the valence of reward (promotion) and the perceived instrumentality of performance for the attainment of the reward. The belief concerning the likelihood that a particular effort, will be followed by a particular first level outcome, is referred to as expectancy in this model. This is the subjective probability or belief concerning the likelihood that a particular action or effort will be followed. Vroom ties the concept of expectancy to person's act by stating that the force on a person to perform an 'action' is a monotonically increasing function of the algebraic sum of the products of the valences of all 'first level' outcomes and the strength of his expectancies that the action will be followed by the attainment of the outcomes (Vroom 1964). Force, here is similar to the concept of motivation. Thus this motivational model exphasises the individual differences in motivation and suggests that it is possible to examine the very explicit relationship between motivation and accomplishment of organizational goals. Different people often have different ideas about expected outcomes, even though the motivation process that activates behaviour remains the same. One employee may equate superior performance with subsequent promotion, while the other employee may relate the satisfactory performance to job security.

Implications for managers in light of Vroom's model are to find out the valued outcomes of employees and to be consistent with the use of these outcomes as the reward or punishment strategies.

In general empirical tests of Vroom's model have shown great potential for predicting behaviour in organizations. Galbraith and Cummings (1967) utilized the model to predict the productivity of industrial workers Five goals namely, fringe, benefits supervisors, support and group acceptance were obtained by graphic rating to measure the instrumentality of performance The study supported

Vroom's model. Christopher (1976) tested the prediction that the amount of values attached to pay is more highly related to job performance, in cases where employees perceive a strong relationship between pay and performance (high instrumentality) than where they preceive a weak one (low instrumentality). In a study of factory supervisors in South Africa, data showed that the correlation between valence and performance in the high instrumentality group was significantly greater than in the low instrumentality group. Data thus support Vroom's model.

This model holds great promise for predicting behaviour in organisations. However, some unanswered questions such as, which goals have definite anticipated satisfaction in work situation, what incremental change in motivation is required to influence the choice of one goal over another and what combination of factors or measures will result in the best prediction of behaviour in a given situation, remain to be investigated (Shrode and Voich, 1974). While using this theory, perhaps, managers would like to know goals that have positive valence in a work situation and how much difference in force is necessary before one kind of outcome is chosen over the other. Further what combination of measures yield best prediction in a given situation (Hunt and Hill 1969). According to Vroom (1964), the most general implications of his model are that occupational choice, job satisfaction and job performance should be regarded as joint functions of individual differences in motives and cognized or actual properties of the work roles. There seems to be important interactions between these two sets of variables.

In the Indian situation, however, we need more insights and data in order to develop a theory of work motivation. Perhaps, values, personality and environmental factors are also important determinants of work motivation. In an attempt to this, few interviews were conducted where good job performers were the subjects of the study.

Presented below are the interviews with some good job performers from Indian industries. They were selected on the purposive basis, just to get an idea about their motivational factors.

Mr. Ashok, an industrial worker of a small scale industry, is 29 years old with ITI diploma. He has been working in this industry for last seven years with a short brake of two months. He is good at engineering, drawing and manufacturing. Perhaps, he tried to get better opportunities and left the job last year, but within a month, he wanted to return to his old job. He is a good worker both technically as well as behaviourally. Therefore, his previous industry took him back without hesitation. His reply to the question, what is motivating for him at the job? He said money of course, is necessary and I had tried to make the change for more money. But soon I realized that the nature of job in that organization was not giving him any opportunity for growth.

Shivraj is 24 years old diploma holder in Mechanical engineering from Bhilai. He has about 20 years of experience. He is good at his job. As a foreman in a mechanical engineering process plant component industries, he is incharge of total manufacturing. The owner of this organisation, also a technocrat, often tries to explain him any new assignment. But he is so confident (some times over confident) that he would say 'Sir, just leave it to me'. He, of course tries hard to deliver the goods, barring a few exceptional situations, he has been quite successful. His excellence in job performance needs his ego boasting to some extent and autonomy freedom to do the job the way he wants to do it. In between he also keeps on suggesting that his emoluments should be increased and others are ready to pay him more. By general market rate he gets higher emoluments in this organization too. However, it looks like that he enjoys his job which has variety, skill, autonomy, responsibility and feedback, all the motivating potential characteristics, suggested by recent job characteristics theory. However, this is coupled with the money factor too.

Mr. Joseph, 48, is a hard working, I.I.T., M. Tech. mechanical engineer with varied experience. He is a superior job performer. However, he has landed up with a research and development centre of a public limited company, which hardly has a research and development activity. As a manager in this organisation, where he gets good salary and performs the best. But he feels frustrated. In his words, two things are most important for any man—a satisfying job and a good-cooperating wife. He is looking for more challenge and variety in his job.

Jagdish is a lathe operator. He has been working for last nine years. Though he does'nt have any degree or diploma in engineering, he has acquired sufficient training and skill for understanding, engineering drawing and operation of this machine. Whenever he performs, he is at his best. However, he takes long leaves very often. This organization has tolerated him because of his good performance,

If absehteism is not a criteria of performance, perhaps he can be considered a good job performer. The reason (we tried to probe into this) is, his land holding and family staying elsewhere which attracts him every now and then.

Romesh is a 27 years old draftsman. Even in such a short career he has made many changes in his job. He came from Calcutta to Faridabad in search of a better job. In Faridabad also, in two years he has changed four jobs, perhaps, he is looking for more challenging job, a good working climate and not really a fat increase in salary. He also does a part time assignment with a highly qualified engineer's machine design job. In this part time job he is working for more than two years. He is quite sincere and enthusiastic about his work. His motivation to better job performance comes from within, the intrinsic motivation.

Mr. Seth has decided to remain in a public sector organisation as a specialist, though he had the choice of becoming general Manager in one of the departments of the organisation. He does not get less salary than the deputy general managers.

But he has no administration powers, no glamour of managerial position. However, he is too good a performer, a perfect engineer and one of the most pleasant personalities. His motivation perhaps comes from within.

By analysing some of the above situations one can say that a number of factors are responsible for performance.. Money perhaps comes towards the last part of the list of these factors, as we have seen that even these industrial workers are looking for better quality of work life through challenge, responsibilty, variety autonomy etc.

Thus, the study presented in this book has taken an approach which tries to study some of the aforesaid factors in combinations. Thus an attempt has been made to develop an alternative model for work motivation.

CHAPTER
SIX

The Conceptual Framework of the Study

MOTIVATION AND JOB PERFORMANCE has received considerable attention in Indian industries in recent years among practising managers, industrial/organizational psychologists and policy makers. This has become focal point of interest, in view of our concern for productivity and effective organizations. For such a concern perhaps, it becomes important for any organization to attract good employees who could perform the task in dependable manner and also use their creativity, innovation in their job performance. On the other hand the organization should give them a working culture, a climate that enhances their growth and fulfils their expectations. Perhaps giving financial incentives, is just one aspect of the whole process. This reasoning gives the feeling that motivational problems are the central theme in the psychology of job performance, leading to effective organizations.

Motivation concept is a highly complex phenomenon that affects and is affected by a large number of factors in the person-organization system. The concept has been defined by many researchers as an inner state that energizes, moves or activates the behaviour of an individual. This has also been defined as a process of governing choices among many forms of activities. In this study, employee's motivation to work has been analysed. An attempt has been made to study the job performance of industrial worker, within the framework of a proposed cognitive theory of work motivation. Such a framework would help us in organizing our thoughts concerning human performance. The conceptual model proposed, makes three assumptions. Firstly, employee motivation for job performance is a complex phenomenon, which cannot be properly understood without a multivariate research design. Secondly, employee perception of the job situation and his expectancies and way of viewing the world is important. Every worker views his work situation through his subjective world. Thirdly, motivationally important factors may be viewed within a system analysis perspective.

Within the multivariate research framework, employee's personality and backward variables have been studied as two groups of factors, and his perception of the organizational climate variables has been studied as the third group of factors.

Cognitive approach to work motivation and the system's approach taken in the study, are explained in the next few pages.

THE ORGANIZATION AS A SYSTEM

The human relations researcher views human behaviour, whether at the individual or at the social level, as developing within an interacting frame-work in which each part influences every other part in a dynamic way. Bakke (1959) defines an organisation as a continuing system which is able to differentiate and integrate human activities which utilize, transform and weld together a set of human material and other resources into a problem solving whole. The function of the organization is to satisfy particular human needs in interaction with other subsystems of human activities in particular environment.

The basic concept was well described by Henderson (1936) who pointed out that the interdependence of the variables in a system is one of the widest inductions (inferences) from experience that we possess, or we may alternatively regard it as a definition of a system. Huse and Bowditch (1973) define the system as a series of interrelated and interdependent parts, such that the interaction of any of the subsystems affects the whole. In fact, systems approach, views interactions and interdependence among subsystems are as important as the individual components. If one of the subsystems malfunctions, it affects the performance of the entire system.

Boulding (1956) has pointed out different levels of system ranging from static structures to cybernetic structures and human systems. He believes that human systems and social systems are the most complicated ones and we have yet to discover the rudiments of theoretical models for them.

An organisation is an open behaviour system with a number of interdependent subsystems. Each subsystem can be considered as a system in its own right as well as a total system. Each worker is one of the important subsystem within the organisation and affects the whole unit in different degrees through his job performance. It is found that the worker, similar to a social system is a complex one in himself consisting of multitude of subsystems acting on inputs, received from outside the world, seeks balance between his desire and need for growth and self-fulfilment.

One may look at the human system from psychological perspective. The important variables are worker's attitude, motivation, values and norms of behaviour, and these will interact with each other. Most of the social systems have multiplicity of subsystems, however, we can select our specific parts or subsystems for study and enlarge our analysis from micro to macro level.

In industrial context some of the motivating factors for good job performance reported, are supervisory style, wages, fringe benefits, working conditions, decision making opportunities, promotional opportunities etc. (Vroom 1964). There seems to be a multiplicity of different sources of satisfaction and dissatisfaction, intrinsic to job performance, which are functions of both, characteristics of the person performing it i.e., his personality (Vroom 1964).

Some of the theories of human motivation in industrial organisations are advanced by Maslow, (1943), Herzberg (1959), and Vroom (1964) which have been discussed earlier.

THE THEORY UNDERLYING THE PRESENT INVESTIGATION

By analysing Maslow's, Herzberg's and Vroom's theories of motivation in industries as related to job performance, the understanding of the concept of job performance seems to rest on the analysis of individual and his interactions with the job situations. How a worker cognises the work situation and himself may form the basis for his job behaviour. The theory underlying the present investigation may as well be labelled as a cognitive theory for understanding the job performance, quite similar to Vroom's and Atkinson's approach. The assumption underlying, the cognitive approach is that the individual's perception of the field is determined by his total personality make up, as it interacts with the environment.

According to Levy (1970), cognitive theories share a basic assumption that a person's behaviour is determined to some degree by his perception and understanding of events. The person is conceived of as an information processing system. Thus, behaviour is considered not as a direct function of external events but of person's interpretations of those events. External reality is not denied by cognitive theorists, but it is seen as entering into the causation of behaviour primarily through its transformation by the person. This transformation is an important aspect in prediction of behaviour. The approach assumes that the stimulus value of both internal and external events depends upon the meaning given by the individual who is actively engaged in their organization and interpretation. In evaluating the support for theoretical formulations of cognitive organisation, Wyer (1974) points out that three classes of variables may affect the reception and acceptance of information. These are characteristics of the situation in which the information is presented, characteristics of the recipient of the information (individual difference variable) and the characteristics of the information itself.

A cognitive approach to motivation places primary emphasis on a person's thought processes. It assumes that people decide what to do on the basis of their evaluations, of the likely outcomes of their behaviour alternatives. Behaviour is the outcome of these decisions. This emphasises that cognitive processing is an important determinant of behaviour. This assumption stands in clear contradiction to the assumption of the mechanistic approach which says that thoughts are not causal factors in behaviour (Deci 1975). Thus, cognitive approach to motivation proposes that people make choices about what to do (Taylor 1960). They act on the basis of their goals and their assessment of various behaviour alternatives which may lead them to these goals. This approach views humans as striving to satisfy their needs by setting goals and choosing behaviour that they believe, will help them to achieve these goals.

According to Levy (1970), contents of cognitive structures, include self concept, expectancies, beliefs etc. People's attitudes, feelings and other internal states, provide information which they use in their decision making. Decisions are also affected by a cognitive representation of the environment. Thus, cognitive approach considers a sequence of events beginning with stimulus inputs and ending with behaviour (Baldwinn 1969, Weiner 1972).

Both, cognitive conceptions and systems approach, view the person as being goal directed and they look inside the mind for ultimate explanation of his behaviour and how he achieves his goals. This is consistent with the idea of an inner locus of causation (Levy 1970). The system conception has important characteristics like organization and orderliness, existence of different entities or sub systems, each with a distinguishing characteristic, and a constantly involved input-output relationship with the environment. Bertalanffy (1950) emphasised that living organisms are not self sufficient. They depend upon their environment for existence. These are referred to as open systems.

Cognitive approach has emerged out of the pioneering work of Tolman (1932) and Lewin (1935, 1951), who first recognised the importance of cognitions as causal factors in behaviour. Lewin was more concerned with social behaviour of human beings and introduced the notion of valence to refer to the psychological value of a particular end state. He also used the term 'goals' and spoke of 'tensions' as the energy source.

Weiner (1972) has proposed that a cognitive model would involve (a) antecedent stimuli (b) mediating cognitive events and (c) behaviour. Lewin's theory emphasised primarily on the link between the last two. The question of needs, according to him would be included in antecedent stimuli aspect of the model. Deci (1975) has stressed that a more complete cognitive theory would focus on the first, as well as on the other characteristics of the model.

Expectancy theories of motivation beginning with the work of Tolman (1932) and Lewin (1935), expanded by Atkinson (1964) and Vroom (1964) focus primarily on expectation about the achievement of goals dealing with later part of the sequence.

Atkinson (1964) has formulated a mathematical relationship between various determinants of achievement behaviour. This model helps in making precise predictions about certain kinds of intrinsically motivated behaviour. Atkinson's theory asserts that the tendency to approach (or avoid) an achievement related situation, is the resultant tendency to approach success and to avoid failure.

One's tendency to approach success is a function of the motives for success, the probability of success and the incentive value of success. Probability of success is one's expectancy of achieving the goal, which is determined from his past experiences. The components of his model are stable achievements related motives and incentives. Reinforcement value of a particular act and individual differences in motives have also been stressed in his 'Expectancy value' theory.

Atkinson (1964) has suggested that psychology of motivation must bring together into a 'single coherent conceptual scheme', the impact on behaviour of the immediate environment, the effect of stable individual differences in personality and the constant influence on behaviour of the persistent under current of active tendencies to bring about a particular effect which can be attributed to past experience.

Both, Vroom's and Atkinson's models, assert that behaviour is in large part, determined by a multiplicative relation between one's expectation about attaining a goal and the valence of that goal. There are, however, differences between the theories. Atkinson's model includes an individual difference component, but in Vrooms model one's achievement motive and other stable factors are not considered directly.

Deci (1975) has emphasised a general theory of motivation which is in line with expectancy theories, but also pays greater attention to the question of antecedents stimuli as emphasised by Weiner (1972). The situation inputs, according to Deci (1975), to the central information processing system, come from three possible sources, 'the external environment, memory and the internal sources.' He has stressed on intrinsically motivated behaviour, which is determined by need for competence and self determination. According to him, the intrinsically motivated activities are ones for which there is no apparent reward except the activity itself. People seem to engage in the activities for their own sake and not because they lead to an extrinsic reward. Deci further points out that a more meaningful definition of intrinsic motivation will iuclude psychological basis of such motivations as the reward for intrinsically motivated activities are mediated within the individual. Koch (1956, 1961) was one of the first to make strong assertions that motivational theory needs to be revamped to give considerable importance to the notion of intrinsic motivation. He emphasised that intrinsically motivated behaviours are highly organised, consequently these should be incorporated in the theories of motivation. Pareek (1974), has suggested that there is a need to have an integrated theory of work motivation and has proposed a three level model of work motivation which includes psychological needs of the individual, need satisfaction in the organization and role satisfaction an individual has in the organization.

JOB PROFORMANCE : A PROPOSED MODEL

The individual's reaction to job situation, his cognition of self and work situation, background factors and skill may be isolated as some sub-systems operating within the system of the employee job performance. Model proposed in this investigation, which includes aforesaid factors, is depicted in Fig. 4. It has partially been tested as a regression model as shown in Fig. 5.

The perception of the job situation has been considered as the attractiveness of the situation as perceived by the worker in terms of his attitudes. An attitude is a predisposition on the part of an individual to evalute some concept, relationship or object in a positive or negative fashion. According to Guilford (1971) an attitude is a personal dispostion common to individuals, but possessed to different degrees which impels them to react to objects, situations, or propositions in ways that can be called favourable or unfavourable. The underlying basis in motivation is responsible for the bipolar nature of an attitude continuum.

Cognitions, thus, are the primary components of attitudes. Katz and Stotland (1959) emphasised that there is a potential relationship between cognitive and affective components of attitude and behaviour. Motivation manifests itself in attitudes and the outcome is behaviour. The perception of job attitudes considered here are comparable to the concept of Valence of Lewin (1938) and Vroom (1964), Atkinson's (1958) incentive and motives, Peak's (1955) attitudes, Maslow's (1943) needs and Herzberg et al's (1959) motivators and Hygeince. For the sake of consistency, the term 'job situation perception' or 'organizational climate perception' has been used throughout the explanation.

Peak (1955) hypothesized that attitudes are related to the ends which serve the object. These attitudes are determined by cognized instrumentality of the object of the attitude for the attainment of

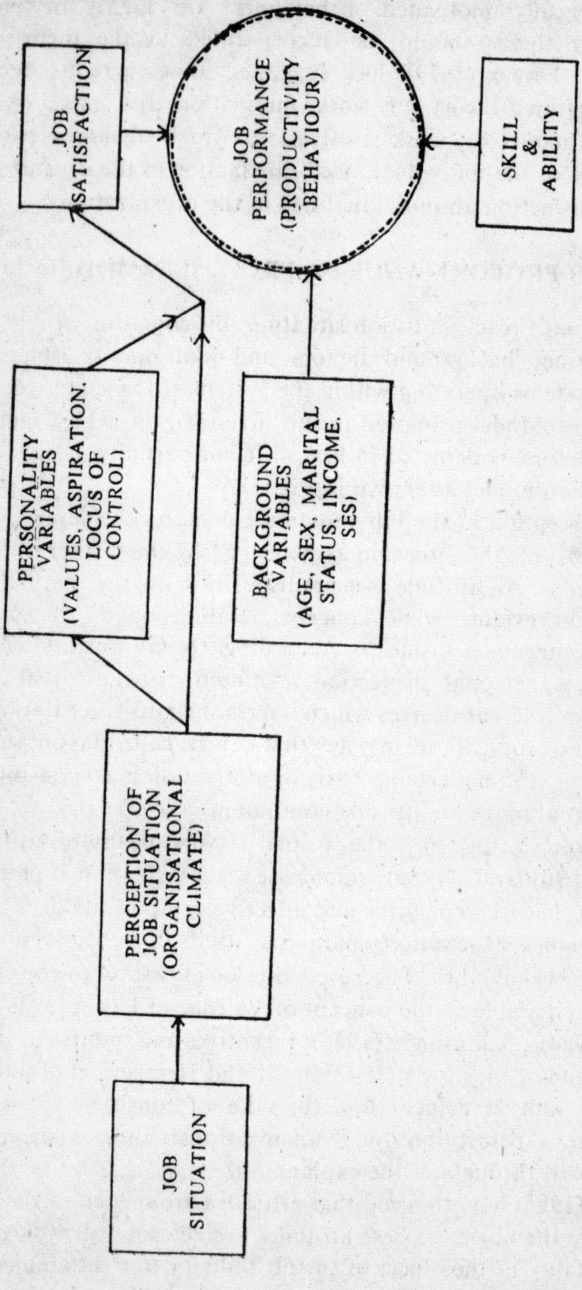

Fig. 4. A Proposed Model of Job Performance.

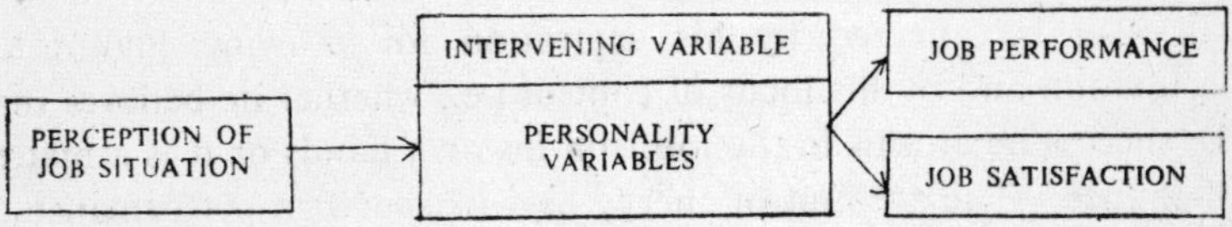

Fig. 5

various consequences as well as the intensity and the nature of the effect expected from these consequences. If an object is believed by a person to lead to desired consequences, the person is predicted to have a positive attitude towards it and vice versa.

Vroom (1964) has emphasized that the specific outcomes attained by a person are dependent not only on the choices he makes but also on the events beyond his control. Thus, the degree to which he believes that these outcomes are probable, also plays an important role in his decision making. This belief is referred to as expectancy (Rotter 1955, 1966; Tolman 1959).

Essentially, when a worker is at the job, first thing is how he perceives the demands of his job. These demands necessarily develop from the essential nature of industrial organization and the type of job it demands from the employee. This is organization's expectation from an individual, it must be perceived and appraised by the worker.

Attractiveness of the Job

Once a worker has perceived what his organization demands from his job or expects from him, he redefines the job according to his personal characteristics. Personal values, perception of different needs, his age, income, sex etc., affect his decision of redifinition of his work roles. Some one with strong need for accomplishment, challenge and growth may take up his job role in a more different way than others. This denotes the valence for a person to perform the job fulfilling different higher level and lower level needs.

Personal Aspiration, Expectancies and Values

How an employee will actually behave in giving a job performance, will also be affected by his aspiration for growing high in his occupation and by his locus of control i.e., whether he believes that the success he attains in the job is in his own hands or it is a matter of chance. The amount of energy he will spend in performance of his job will thus depend on his generalized expectancy coupled with attractiveness of different facets of job situations.

Job Performance

Actual work behaviour i.e., job performance is likely to result from a combination of motivational forces discussed above, moderated by skill and abilities. Even a well-executed plan of job performance is doomed to failure if workers do not have skill and potential for the job.

Both, performance outcomes and job satisfaction may be affected by aforesaid factors and may be affecting each other.

This model (Fig. 4) depicts a few internal and external motivating factors which could be determinants of job performance in industrial organizations, in the light of congnitive approach, emphasised in this investigation.

The model has been partially tested as a regression model as shown in Fig. 5. This model emphasizes whether job situation variables or personality variables, account for a major proportion of variance (alone or together) predicting job performance, indicating whether personality dispositions act as intervening variables.

A Causal Model of Job Performance

This causal model has been tested by regression analysis predicting both, job performance and job satisfaction.

Researches related to these factors and the development of the hypotheses are presented in Chapter VII.

Thus, following variables were included in the present investigation.

Background Variables :

1. Age
2. Sex
3. Total experience

4. Length of present tenure
5. Marital status
6. Affiliation to labour unions
7. Socio-economic status
8. Income.

Personality Variables :

1. Level of occupational aspiration
2. Values
3. Internal locus of control
4. Intelligence.

Attitudes of the Workers Towards :

1. Financial benefits
2. Working environment
3. Self esteem and consideration
4. Self development opportunity
5. Closeness of supervision
6. Job security
7. Feeling of belongingness
8. Communication and interaction opportunities
9. Over-all organizational climate.

Organizational Variables :

1. Ownership of the industries
2. Size of the industries
3. Job satisfaction.

Job Performance Variables :

1. Productivity (quality+quantity of work)
2. Co-operativeness
3. Obedience and behaviour towards superiors
4. Initiative
5. Objective estimate of production data. (if available).

The variables are discussed in greater details along with the hypotheses in the next chapter.

CHAPTER
SEVEN

Hypotheses : The Logic and Development

INDUSTRIAL ORGANIZATIONS, though commonly characterised by their physical structure, are psycho-social systems. An industrial organization functions successfully only when the people filling each structural position, perform their roles in a dependable manner. Behaviour of a skilled worker within an organizational setting represents an interaction between the behavioural demands of the task situation and the behavioural requirements that the individual has for himself. Thus, given a job, there are a variety of questions that one can ask about his accomplishment and effectiveness at the job. Survey of the studies reported, reveal that job performance is a result of many inter-related and complex set of variables. It is thus necessary to explore total situation in assessing this job linked behaviour as far as possible as already discussed in the conceptual framework for the study and depicted in the model.

ABILITY AND MOTIVATION AS JOINT DETERMINANTS OF PERFORMANCE

According to Vroom (1964), job performance is a result of ability multiplied by motivation. This assumption has led to efforts to measure abilities and motivation as determinants of job performance. Term "ability" usually denotes a potential for performing some task. A person's ability to perform a task refers to the degree to which he possesses all the psychological attributes necessary for a high level of performance excluding those of motivational nature. Vroom (1960) reported high positive correlation between ability and performance of those higher in motivation, and zero or slightly negative correlations for those low in it.

French (1957) studied the joint effects of intelligence and achievement motivation on problem solving success of airmen and found a significant interaction between these variables. Among those subjects who were high in motivation, performance was positively related to their intelligence. Fleishman (1958) had concluded on the basis of a study conducted on airforce trainees that performance was significantly higher under high motivation condition than under low. However, the difference in performance between the two motivation conditions was significantly greater for subjects high in ability (as measured by previous performance on the task).

Vitles (1953) used the terms like "capacity to work" and "will to work" and had proposed that both determine the level of performance. Muthayya (1962) studied intelligence of high and low achievers in the scholastic field in a group of 30 boys and found a lack of relationship between achievement and intelligence. Vroom (1964) has suggested that if an interaction between ability and motivation were to be corroborated in further research, it would have considerable implications for managerial practice.

In the present study, occupational skills and education have been kept constant by selecting the skilled workers with specialised industrial training diploma (ITI). Intelligence as a variable has also been included in the study. It is hypothesised that :

HYPOTHESIS I

(*i*) Intelligence of the worker is related to the level of job performance.

(*ii*) Good and poor job performers will show a significant difference in their intelligence.

RELATIONSHIP OF MOTIVATION TO PERSONALITY

The way a given motive is manifested in behaviour is a function of the particular personality constellation in which it is embedded (Cofer and Appley 1964). Expressions of the attitudes are influenced by many variables including motivation and personality. Klein

(1954) has used the concept of 'cognitive control' to refer to a manner or style of performance which reflects in a number of situations. Perhaps the effects of any motive are filtered through the constraint provided by personality controls. This is to say that controls in a subject's personality will moderate the way he responds to a need and the way motive is reflected in behaviour. Such findings suggest that to trace out motivational effects in behaviour of people, the personality and other variables must be taken into consideration. According to Cofer and Appley (1964), the expression of motivation in adult human being is modulated in all probability by personality mechanism, so that the direct evidence of motivational factors is seldom seen.

No two persons have exactly the same mixture or strength of these needs and personality. There are some people who are driven mainly by money, others are primarily concerned with security, and so on. While individual differences must be recognised, it does not mean that, predictions about the motive which seems to be currently more prominent among employees cannot be made (Hersey and Blanchard 1974). They further point out that individuals act on the basis of their perceptions and not on reality. By bringing reality and their perception closer, a manager can increase the effectiveness of the employees.

Motivation, embedded in workers' personality, background characteristics and attitudes may affect the employee job performance. Present investigation throws light mainly on some background, psychological and attitudinal variables as related to job performance, Apart from these random variables, a fixed variable, *i.e.*, the ownership of the company (private or public sector) has also been included in the study.

BACKGROUND VARIABLES

Relationship between an individual's demographic characteristics and job performance may suggest that people with similar background have similar behaviour structure. Herman and Hulin (1972) demonstrated that, within the same organization, demographic background accounted for a significant and substantial portion of the variance in responses to the work environment. Background factors included in this study are age, experience, sex, marital status, tenure in the present organization, socio-economic status and income.

Age : Herzberg et al (1959) suggest that the younger men more frequently perceived the intrinsic characteristics of the work itself as a reason for lack of motivation than older ones in their sample. In general, older group reported high morale. Sinha and Agrawal (1971) concluded that older workers had better job motivation than younger ones. Herman Dunham and Hulin (1975) reported that older employees who were the primary wage earners in their families appeared to have high level of job involvement. This study identified young male employees as being less satisfied with supervisor and experiencing low level of job involvement and motivation. Taylor (1975) examined the influence of age on performance in decision making on a sample of industrial managers. Age was found to influence the performance in decision making.

Sex : House (1974) found that, when females were in competitive situation, they showed lower expectancies for their performances than did males. Deaus and Emswiller (1974) reported that good performance by females are more likely to be attributed to luck. Similar results are reported by Feldman, Summers and Kiesher (1974) in a study of attribution of occupational success. Matteson and Mc Mohan (1974) reported significant differences between the two sexes as regards to their job attitudes. Frieze (1975) also found that there are differences in causal attributions for success and failure in males and females.

Men generally attribute their success to stable factors such as ability, and failure to luck. Pattern is reverse in case of women. This relationship, however, is moderated by individual differences in achievement motivation. These findings may have implications for job performance as well.

With the dual role of career making and home making for women, it is quite likely that need patterns and motivational forces influencing job performance may not follow same pattern for males and females. In recent years, in India, with possible entry of women on industrial scene, this concept becomes more interesting. This field has not been probed deeply in the Indian context.

Pay and Income : Generally, managers feel that pay is the most important aspect of job motivation. Herzberg's theory (Herzberg et al. 1959) stresses its role as hygiene factor, although Lawler

(1973) indicates that it can serve as a motivator of job performance.

Earlier, Whyte (1955) stressed that there is no doubt that money has an important effect on behaviour of production workers, but this effect is neither as simple nor as strong as management has often assumed.

Gellerman (1967) emphasized that an individual's reaction to income prospects is more consistent with his sense of competence.

In view of the contradictory findings on impact of money as a motivator to job performance, this variable has been included in the study.

Experience : Experiences are cumulative learning in the sense that each new situation is inevitably dealt with in terms of previous experience. Past experience usually assists in the new working situation of the similar type improving the speed and accuracy of dealing with the job resulting in better accomplishment of job. But the relationship does not seem to be just and simple.

Kohn and Schooler (1973) studied the relationship between man's occupational experience and his psychological functioning and suggested that these results from a continuing interplay between job and man, in which the effects of job on man are far from trivial.

Socio-economic status : Study of socio-economic status has become important with shift of workers from rural to urban industrialised cities in India. It is only after India's independence that Industrial townships have started coming up, transforming nearby villages into town. Generally, farm workers have changed their occupation and have joined the industrial force. Such a transformation in society has certainly made impact on the socio-economic status of the industrial workers. This fact is likely to make some reflection on the job performance of the workers.

Tenure in present organization : Tenure in the corporation according to Herman, Dunham and Hulin (1975) is descriptive of the direct employee-organization interface. Thus, this background variable may influence employee motivation in terms of job performance.

Marital status : Herman, Dunham and Hulin (1975) found that persons with similar demographic characteristics like age, sex and marital status reported similar degree of satisfaction and job involvement, and experienced similar levels of motivation. The unique relationship between demographic characteristics and psychological responses suggests that employees perceive work experience through the lence of their own value system.

Thus it has been hypothesized that :

HYPOTHESIS II

(*i*) Certain background variables like age, experience, tenure, sex etc., are related to the level of job performance.

(*ii*) Male and female workers show different relationships between these variables.

(*iii*) Workers in public and private sector industries have different pattern of correlations between these variables.

(*iv*) Workers in high and low levels of job performance groups differ as regards to these background variables.

ATTITUDES TOWARDS ORGANIZATION AND ORGANIZATIONAL CLIMATE

Attitudes are the tendencies to respond positively or negatively towards any person, object or situation. According to Guilford (1971), motivations are manifested in attitudes. This being so, the knowledge of attitudes may help in the prediction of behaviour in industry. Attitudes are related to values, internal needs, level of aspirations, expectations and motivations of the individual worker.

According to Herzberg et al. (1959), the problem of people's relationship with their work continues to be a basic one and attitudes towards the job exert an extremely important influence on the way the job was done.

Evan (1976) has emphasized the importance of attitudes as organizational climate perception. According to him, organizational climate is a multidimensional perception by members as well as non-members of the essential attributes or character of an organizational system.

He further points out that organizational members tend to perceive the climate differently and this perception whether real or unreal has behavioural consequences for the organization.

Lawler (1968) examined the relationship between expectancy attitude and job performance. The model relates motivation, ability, reward and performance. The study revealed that managerial expectancy attitudes were strongly related to superior ratings of performance by supervisors.

Organizational climates according to Meglino (1976) are uniformities of perceived attributes within the organization or their sub-systems. Camball et al. (1970) view that, for an individual member within an organization climate takes the form of a set of attitudes and expectations which describe the organization in terms of both static characteristics (such as degree of autonomy) and behaviour-outcome contingencies. Of particular interest in their study is the approach that the critical elements of organizational climate were individual perceptions of the organization and these perceptions governed his behaviour. Climate itself was viewed as a situational variable. Studies tend to show a consistent relationship between organizational climate and job satisfaction, but the link between climate and job performance has been unclear.

Hellriegel and Slocum (1974) state that the relationship between job performance and climate is not as easily understood as the relationship between job satisfaction and organization climate.

Studies drawing opposite conclusions regarding the relationship involving job performance and organizational climate have further complicated the issue. Hall and Lawler (1969) concluded that high producing organizational units tend to be viewed as dominant rather than submissive; hard, rather than soft; and competitive, rather than co-operative. In contrast, Friedlander and Greenberg (1971) showed that effective organizational behaviour was associated with a supportive climate.

Meglino (1976) further stresses that an evaluative climate can enhance the performance at well learned tasks while retarding it at poorly learned tasks. Using this relationship, he views that a series of research studies which at first seem unrelated or even contradictory can be connected in a unified thread of conclusions. He also emphasized that organizational climate and its relationship to job performance has not been fully explored.

In the present investigation, organizational climate has been considered as a perceptual measure in terms of attitudes and need satisfaction opportunities in the organization.

Variables included in this study are financial benefits, supervision, self development opportunities, feeling of belongingness, working conditions, employment security, contribution and participation opportunities, interaction opportunities, job satisfaction and perception of the overall organizational climate. Apart from this, a few organizational climate constructs like administration are also included. According to Mitchell (1976), the general notion in industry regarding motivation is that managers must motivate their employees. Actually it works the other way round; motivation results from the urge within a person to do something, to accomplish a task, to reach a goal. At the most, managers can provide a climate which will nourish the growth of motivation within workers.

Explanations related to some of these organizational climate factors are given in the following pages.

Supervision

It is frequently suggested that consideration by a supervisor for his subordinates has positive effect on their motivation to perform the task effectively. Davis (1962) concluded that employee oriented supervisors tend to get better productivity and worker motivation. Likert (1959) asserts that supervisors who are supportive, friendly, helpful and considerate towards their subordinates, obtain high outputs.

Katz, Maccoby and Morse (1950) indicated that there was substantial difference in the amount of consideration that low and high producing unit supervisors showed to their subordinates. Highly productive supervisors were typically characterised as employee centred.

Decision Making Opportunities

Association of workers with the management of industrial enterprises is being increasingly realised as an effective means of ensuring industrial peace and maximising productivity. Participation of workers in decision making not only helps in reducing tensions but also brings best out of them.

Mulder (1971) holds workers' participation in decision making as important motivational determinant of output and workers' effectiveness. Saiyaddin (1971) has also pointed out the importance of decision making opportunities as motivating force in industries. Participation of workers in decision making is assumed to result not only in greater satisfaction, but also in higher productivity (Scott 1962, Davis 1962). Lawrence and Smith (1955) carried out an experiment and found that work groups making a decision concerning production goals attained higher productivity than those who just took part in group discussion.

According to Vroom (1964), workers' participation can increase worker's "ego involvement" in decision. This can as well give fulfilment of self esteem needs to the worker. In India, workers' participation in industrial organization is a new concept. This needs to be investigated.

Financial Benefits

Financial benefits like wages, bonus and fringe benefits are almost universal forms of inducement to industrial workers. While investigating factors related to job performance, one point of view is that the strength of worker's motivation to perform effectively is directly related to the amount of his wages. More money he receives, higher is his motivation to perform his job. Vroom (1964) writes that there is no reliable data indicating that increase in wages increases level of performance.

Georgopoulos, Mahoney and Jones (1957) have thrown light on individual differences in performance of workers on an individual wage incentive plan. They reported a larger proportion of 'high producers' among workers who perceived that productivity would result in their receiving more money in the long run than those who reported that productivity was either irrelevant to, or hindered the attainment of money. In the light of Vroom's model (1964), if there is positive valence for money, we would predict that the valence of effective performance on a job would be directly related to the instrumentality of performance for its attainment. According to Herzberg et al. (1959) salary has more potency as a job dissatisfier than as satisfier.

Gallerman (1967) stated that there is no doubt that money has an important effect on the thinking and behaviour of production worker, but this effect is neither as simple nor as strong as managements have often assumed.

Working Conditions

Working conditions include factors like hours of work, tools, canteen facility, ventilation etc. These are important factors which may give more physical comfort to the worker. Herzberg et al.

(1959) reported that working condition was rarely instrumental in bringing about high motivation.

Employment Security

According to Maslow (1943), security, stability, freedom from fear etc., denote security needs and may be strong motivator in the industrial context; generally fear of unemployment and retrenchment may be viewed as desire for security. This feeling is likely to be related to workers' job performance.

Interaction Opportunities

Interaction opportunities and communication patterns are in fact important motivating forces in organizational life Mulder (1960) and Shaw (1954) have explored the effects of organizational structure on individuals task performance. In the present investigation, how individual worker perceives the interaction opportunities within the organization has been taken into account and how they are related to their job performance.

Perception of Opportunities for the Self Esteem and Self Development

Desire for achievement, self respect, self esteem, trust in one's desire for self fulfilment and tendency to become actualised in what one is capable of, are the higher order needs according to Maslow (1943). Workers perceiving such opportunities within the organization may be better at job performance. Porter (1963) found that top executives are more concerned with self esteem and self actualization than the lower level staff. Hall and Nougaim (1968) reported that, for managers, the need for esteem increases over the years of tenure, and esteem and achievement become significantly greater for successful managers.

Feeling of Belongingness

Likert (1953) found that work groups with high group loyalty are more productive. They have greater feeling of belongingness and have the better interpersonal relations. Schein (1970) has stressed upon the social nature of man as of primary importance in workplace and viewed this as a dominant factor in determining his job performance. According to him, man is basically motivated by social needs, and obtains his basic sense of identity through relationship with others. He further points out that man is more responsive to the social forces of the peer group than incentives, and he is responsive to the management only to the extent he feels that his social needs of belongingness and acceptance are met. Maslow (1943) has also stressed the importance of need for belongingness in industrial motivation.

HYPOTHESIS III

(*i*) Positive attitudes of the workers towards fringe and financial benefits, working conditions, supervision, feeling of belongingness, self development opportunities, communication and interaction emphasis are related to the job performance of the workers.

(*ii*) Male and female workers show different types of relationships between their attitudes and job performance.

(*iii*) Workers in Public and Private sector industries will show different relationships between their attitudes and job performance.

(*iv*) Workers in good and poor job performance groups differ in their job attitudes.

It was also hypothesised that :

HYPOTHESIS IV

(*i*) Scores based on the perception of the organisational climate will be related to the level of job performance

(*ii*) Extreme groups of job performers differ in organisational climate perceptions.

SOME PERSONALITY CORRELATES OF JOB PERFORMANCE

Behaviour is governed not by objective facts, but by the facts as perceived by individuals. According to Stagner (1956), each person sees the world in a manner slightly more different than others. These differences are results of unique individual personality and psychological make up. A job which is satisfying and motivating to one person may often be boring to others. Individual differences in need strengths may be related to some personality characteristics of the workers result in different motivations.

Saunders and Stanton (1976) attempted to find unique patterns of personality traits which are associated with various performance styles. Using cannonical correlation analysis three separate performance styles were extracted with sets of personality traits. Authors concluded that concern should be placed on their psychological set since it plays important role in their process of goal attainment.

In this investigation, locus of control, values and occupational aspirations have been studied as variables related to job performance and as intervening variables between perception of organisational climate and job performance.

Locus of Control : Locus of control (Rotter 1966) is a personality dimension related to an individual's attempt to master the environment. In the framework of Rotter's (1966) social learning theory, internal-external locus of control refers to the degree to which an individual perceives success and failure as being contingent upon personal initiative. At one end of the internal-external continuum are the highly internals, i.e., those who perceive effort to be largely instrumental in attaining success. At the other end of the spectrum are the highly, externals those who attach no values to initiative, and view the success as completely uncorrelated to ability and efforts. Internals thus believe that they control the fate, whereas externals feel that they are controlled by it.

Although the literature on internal-external control has given little attention to this variable as it relates to job performance, the construct is particularly well suited for predicting employment success and job performance. Research studies reported by Joe (1971), Lefcourt (1966, 1972) and Rotter (1966, 1972) contain strong evidence that an internal expectancy reflects a propensity to influence one's environment. Internals believe that success results from hard work. Lefcourt (1972) considers this factor as offering considerable support for a theoretically provable relationship between effectiveness and increased perceptions of personal controls. Inspite of voluminous literature on locus of control, not many research efforts have been made to explore the role of this variable in the dynamics of work experience. Broedling (1975) studied relationship between job performance and locus of control. His hypothesis that internal locus of control will be related to the work motivation and job performance were confirmed at .05 significance level.

Andrisoni and Nestel (1976) examined the influence of internal-external control on a number of facets of work experience. The study concluded that data provided considerable support for the hypothesis that success at work enhances the expectancy of internal controls. Noditch and Demaio (1975) studied relationship between locus of control and effective performance in schools. Results indicated that, among males, locus of control was significantly related to competent performance only among those subjects who placed a high value on outcome in each area. Among females the pattern was exactly the reverse.

LEVEL OF OCCUPATIONAL ASPIRATIONS

How the individual sets his goal and reacts to his own performance is an important factor determining prediction of his job success. The process of goal setting, or the level of aspiration was first emphasised by Lewin (1935). A quite widely accepted generalization from experiments on level of aspiration is that successful performance leads to an increased level of aspiration and unsuccessful one leads to reduced level (Lewin et. al. 1944); (Child and Whiting, 1949).

There are probably differences among situations in the ways in which various factors influence subjective probabilities on the hand, and incentive values on the other. The value of a given incentive may vary as a function of various group standards, or personality factors. Vroom (1964) stated that there have been no such investigations in industrial situations.

Values

Values play a central role in our lives; a good deal of our behaviour is based upon values we hold. Every decision we make contains both factual and value elements. Workers in industry also behave in accordance with how they perceive the job situation. According to Krech, Churchfield and Ballachery (1962), people construct a "cognitive image or map" of their world. Behaviour is the result of such perceptions.

Bertalanffy (1964) pointed out that values are things or acts which are chosen by and are desirable to an individual within the certain frame of reference. He further points out that we obviously will have to include both objects and acts while studying value patterns. Material things like dollars or a Picasso painting and the charitable acts also stress different values. These preferences affect the behaviour of an individual.

Tolman (1951) stressed on belief-value matrix, which may be culturally shared or unique to an individual. It consists of beliefs that doing things or getting to objects, situations, or goals, will gain satisfaction. These belief-value systems are acquired through experience and may function as an instrumentality in the service of needs.

Littman (1958) refers to value as a motivational term, because it designates something that is active rather than passive. Measured values and preferences have practical utility in predicting other behaviour (Coffer and Appley 1964).

Value, according to Vroom (1964), refers to preference like valence; but it is broader in nature and refers to the strength of desires or aversions for iarge classes of outcomes. In this study Allport-Vernon-Lindzey (1951) scale of values has been used. This scale, based on spranger's classification of values, provides data on six value dimensions; theroetical, economical, social, religious, aesthetic and political, Vernon and Allport (1931) compared the scores on Allport-Vernon value scale of persons working in different fields and found that, in general, these groups were congruent with the nature of their chosen professions. Though the construct suggested by Allport-Vernon-Lindzey has been used as a motivational force in many fields it has not been studied generally with reference to employee job performance in industries.

According to Sikula (1971), values and value systems are merely priority patterns of values along a continuum of importance. More insightful analysis of motivated behaviour can be made via the use of value concept. He further points out that study of value is a new and promising approach to explain motivated behaviour. Value analysis can be used to understand not only individual behaviour but group and organizational behaviour as well. Therefore, it has been hypothesised as follows :

HYPOTHESIS V

(*i*) Certain personality variables like level of occupational aspiration, locus of control and value patterns are related to the level of job performance.

(*ii*) Male and female workers show different patterns of relationship among these variables.

(*iii*) Workers in public and private industries show different pattern of relationship between their personality variables and job performance.

(*iv*) Workers in good job performance group will be different from those in poor job performance group as regards to their value profiles.

JOB SATISFACTION AND JOB PERFORMANCE

The extent to which a worker strives to perform effectively in a job, is not solely a function of his personality or of the nature of his work role but is a complex resultant of both types of variables. The argument, that worker's satisfaction and his motivation to perform effectively should be viewed as a joint function of situational and personality variables, by no means implies that their determinants are identical (Vroom 1964). Generally, very low correlation between job performance and job satisfaction reported in researches also throws light on this issue. Katz, Maccoby and Morse (1950) and Katz, Maccoby, Gurin and Floor (1951) reported no relationship between job performance and job satisfaction. Brayfield and Crockett (1955) concluded that there was a little evidence of any simple or appreciable relationship between employee attitude and job performance. Landy (1969), Pritchard (1969), Comisarow (1970) and Huber (1970) in their various studies have analysed variables like motivations, superior-subordinate relationship and challenge in relation to job satisfaction and job performance. They observed that such variables did not show similar pattern of relationship to job satisfaction and job performance.

Korman (1968) found that subject's self esteem moderated the relationship between task success (performance) and task likes (satisfaction). Vecchio (1980) has indicated that moderator hypothesis is valid for worker anomie, education and type of residence.

Hulin (1971) and Hackman and Lawler (1971) have demonstrated that job satisfaction and other favourable outcomes are primarily characteristics of those who desire satisfaction of higher order needs. This motivational moderator appears to provide for more precise prediction than moderators of sociological nature.

HYPOTHESIS VI

In predicting employee productivity, attitudes, showing perception of higher order need satisfaction will have intervening effect of personality variables, and generally job situation factors will account for a major portion of variance.

HYPOTHESIS VII

(*i*) There is a high relationship between job satisfaction and productivity.

(*ii*) Level of productivity and job satisfaction can be predicted from the set of variables.

It was further hypothesized that :

HYPOTHESIS VIII

Background variables, personality variables and attitudes can predict job performance.

OWNERSHIP OF INDUSTRY

In India, after independence, the entry of government in industrial field created a new class of industry called 'Public Sector Undertaking'.

The employees have tremendous job security. Seniority is perhaps one of the main criterion for promotion. It is likely that motivating factors viewed by workers in these set-ups may differ from those in private sector.

Newstrom, Relief and Monezka (1976) stated that the U.S. public has long held a number of stereotypes about the nature of Government employees as compared to private ones particularly with regard to their motivation and job performance. Some of the points emphasised in this study are that public employees place greater value on security than the employees in private firms. Public employees have less concern for self actualization and they are more dissatisfied with their fringe benefits than private employees.

Public employees are more dissatisfied with their level of economic reward. The study was conducted to provide new insights into organizational reward system. Implications in their study are that self actualization must be created and continuing attention must be paid to recognising and dealing positively with the changing nature of employee needs.

In India, generally, all public sector units are large in size i.e., employing more than 1000 employees, whereas private industries, generally, do not have such strength barring few exceptions. Size of an industry may also have an impact on the employee job satisfaction, job performance and personality. Harrell (1971) reported that men in small business had higher compensation, were better satisfied with their jobs and participated more broadly in management than those in larger companies (of 1000 or more employees).

Therefore, in all the above hypotheses, a corollary has been added about the employees in public and private sector organizations.

Data have been collected by a survey. Design of the study is presented in the next section.

CHAPTER
EIGHT

Design of the Study

As suggested in the earlier chapters on the conceptual framework and variables included in the study, survey research design, seems most appropriate for a study like this. Except for the intelligence test data were collected through interviews and questionnaires.

DATA COLLECTION AND ANALYSIS

Method

After pretesting, data were collected from 14 industrial units from Faridabad, Bhopal and Hardwar. Questionnaires and interviews were used as methods for data collection. The experimenter always had, face to face, contact with subjects and helped them to overcome any difficulty encountered in replying. Workers were tested either individually or in small groups of three at a time depending upon the convenience of the industry concerned. They were assured of the confidentiality of their responses. Questionnaires were collected directly by the investigator. The average testing time was two and a half hours, through some workers needed three and a half hours also. As an incentive each worker was presented with a ball pen.

Description of tests and inventories used, sampling, population characteristics, and data analysis are presented here.

TESTS AND INVENTORIES USED IN DATA COLLECTION

(i) Background Variables

(*a*) *Biodata* : Biodata blank was used for this purpose. Information regarding age, sex, experience, present tenure, marital status, affiliation to labour union etc., was collected.

(*b*) *Socio-Economic Status* : *SES* was measured by SESSQ Urban scale (Jalota, Pandey, Kapoor, Singh 1970). The scale includes components like parental occupation, education of brothers and sisters or children, income, type of house, material possession in the house, cultural level of the family as judged by the expenditure on newspapers, magazines etc. The scale also includes psychological indicators like level of occupational aspiration and concept of social prestige.

Test-retest reliability of the scale is reported in the manual to be .89 (N=50) after one month interview.

(ii) Personality Variables

(*a*) *Values* : Values were measured by Allport, Vernon, Lindzey (1951) scale of values. The scale includes six dimensions of values, i.e., social, religious, economic, theoretical, political and aesthetic values. The scale gives a comparative estimate of preference of values. The scale is self administering, without any time limit and may be applied to individuals or small groups.

The split-half reliability of the scale reported in the manual for the revised form is as follows :

(N=100)

Theoretical Value	.73
Economic Value	.87
Aesthetic Value	.80
Social Value	.82
Political Value	.77
Religious Value	.90

(*b*) *Locus of Control* : This variable was measured by Rotter's IE scale (Rotter 1966). The scale consists of items indicating internal and external locus of control of the subjects. In this 29 paired items scale they have to respond to one of these two items, indicating their belief about the nature of the world.

Split-half reliability of the scale reported in the manual is .65 (N=50) and Spearman-Brown reliability as .79 (N=50). Test-retest reliability of the Hindi Version after two months interval was computed to be .66 (N=39).

(*c*) *Level of Occupational Aspiration* : For measuring the level of occupational aspiration of the industrial workers, a three level occupational aspiration scale was constructed. Workers were asked to indicate the position they wanted to attain in life out of the given list of positions. The first stage consisted of the positions such as chief engineer, chief executive, managing director of a firm, a high official and owner of an industry. Workers aspiring for any of these positions were put in the group of high level of aspiration. The second stage included positions of supervisor, junior level executive or a work-shop owner. The third stage included mechanic, skilled worker, salesman etc.

A score of 3 was allotted to the worker aspiring for the highest level of aspiration, 2 for the second stage and 1 for the lowest level of occupational aspiration.

Reliability : Test-retest reliability of these responses has been computed to be .90 with an interval of two months between the test and retest sessions.

(*d*) *Intelligence* : IPAT culture fair intelligence test Scale II by Cattell and Cattell (1960) was used for getting an indication of intelligence.

(*e*) *Organizational climate attitudes* : Attitudes towards various aspects of organizational climate were measured by a factor analysed Organizational Climate Questionnaires (OCDQ) for industries (Sharma and Mathur 1982). This is a Likert type Scale with 36 items. These items have been discussed under eight factors in a varimax rotated factor analysis. The factors are :

1. Spirit, warmth and support
2. Security
3. Working conditions
4. Self development
5. Administration
6. Self-esteem and consideration
7. Communication and interaction
8. Supervision

The scale includes both the positive and the negative items, which are scored differently.

The reliability (test-retest) is computed to be .891 after a gap of two months between sessions (N=39).

In each factor a number of questions have been grouped mathematically. These questions have been used as the score for that particular attitude towards organization. The attitude towards organizations and a total index of the organizational climate perception has been used in the analysis.

(*f*) *Job Satisfaction* : Job satisfaction was inferred from the interview schedule developed for this study. Test-retest reliability of these responses is computed to be .78 (N=39) with an interval of two months between the test and retest sessions.

(*g*) *Job Performance Criteria* : Since no such job performance schedule was available which could be used for all types of industries, specially in batch production factories, a job performance appraisal form was developed exclusively for this study. Views of twenty one managers in Indian Industries and existing literature in this field, served as the basis for the development of the criteria. Next Chapter IX throws light on the development of job performance criteria. In the mass production industries objective data were also gathered for productivity.

(*h*) *Organizational Variables* : Data regarding the size of the organization, its product, ownership and company policy were gathered from the personnel managers or concerned departments in the organizations.

SAMPLING AND POPULATION CHARACTERISTICS

Faridabad, a leading industrial city on the outskirts of Delhi, established after independence of India, was chosen as the field for this study for private sector industries.

Faridabad Industrial Complex ranks as one of the topmost industrial centres in the country. The growth of this area has been spectacular. There are more than 1000 industries operating in the city producing wide variety of goods. (Directory of Faridabad Industries 1972).

For the purpose of this study only industries with more than 50 regular employees were listed out. This reduced the number to 142 industries. Finally, 12 industries were included in the study by simple random sampling procedure (Kish 1965). These industries are of varying sizes and products (Appendix A). A second stage of sampling was done at every industry to choose the skilled workers who were to participate in this study. During the year data were collected, the industries were facing acute shortage of electrical power. This had put them financially in a bad shape. They, obviously, were reluctant to further waste the productive time of workers by allowing them to participate in this kind of survey. However, after a good deal of persuasion, the authorities in most of the selected industries had very kindly agreed to spare 10% to 15% of their workers for this purpose.

As the entry of women in industries in India has started only recently, number of women workers remain meagre. Therefore, in each industry women were sampled separately to get the true representation of women workers.

It was observed that this industrial complex does not have any manufacturing unit which is a public sector undertaking.

Entry of Government in industrial field has given new impetus to industrialisation in India. In these industries, which are generally large, workers seem to have different values than in smaller organizations owned by private owners. All these companies are large in size with generally more than 1000 employees each. There is no concentration of industries owned by government at one place. They are situated in all parts of the country.

For the purpose of comparison it was decided to include a large public sector industries in the study. Two units of a public sector organization producing power plant equipment like turbines, generators, motors, switch-gears etc. were included in the study.

In both, private and public sector industries, only the employees working in day shift were included in the study. Final sampling design, was a two stage stratified simple random sampling method, in private sector, and stratified simple random sampling in two plants of public sector industry (Kish 1965).

Data were collected from 139 workers from public sector undertakings and 258 workers from private sector, making the total sample N=397. There were 353 male workers, whereas only 44 female workers could be included in the sample.

The brake-up of 397 subjects into sub-samples, is as follows :

	Public Sector	*Private Sector*	*Total*
Males	128	225	353
Females	11	33	44
Total	139	258	397

Average age of the workers was 27.32 years. They were categorised as skilled workers by industries, mostly with ITI (industrial training institute) diploma. They made experience ranging from one to 15 years, were belonging generally to different socio-economic and marital-status. The industries included in the sample range in size from 50 to more than 10,000 employees producing a variety of items such as chemicals, pharmaceuticals, light engineering goods, tractors, heavy electrical equipments, textiles, electronics etc. (Appendix A).

STATISTICAL ANALYSIS

Data were analysed using univariate, bivariate and multivariate methods of analysis. First, the computations were done for the total sample. Another analysis was carried out with a brake up of public and private sector industries. Data on males and females were also analysed separately. Product moment correlations for all the variables in all sub-groups and the total sample were computed.

Multivariate statistical methods are emphasised because they make it possible to encompass all the data from an investigation in one analysis. This approach results in a clearer and better organised account of the investigation than does the piecemeal analysis of the data in parts. It also yields more realistic probability estimate in hypothesis testing than to separate partial analysis. Kendall (1957), emphasises that the variates are interdependent among themselves so that we cannot split one or more from the others and consider one by itself. Thus, variates must be considered together.

According to Boek (1975), behavioural research typically involves problems in which several response variables are observed simultaneously which necessitates the use of multivariate analysis.

Wood (1971) also emphasized that the item weight of discriminant function analysis, was most effective in distinguishing the extreme groups,

In this study, a stepwise regression analysis has been used with job performance as a criterion variable to get the composite weightage of each of the other variables on job performance (for total sample).

In stepwise regression, a likely single independent variable is related to the dependent variable through a regression equation. Then other dependent variables are added, one at a time. If their partial coefficients show that they make a significant contribution, they are kept in the equation, if not, they are dropped and the new independent variables are tested (Jedamus, Frame and Taylor 1976). A stepwise procedure, thus, allows the data to tell their own story in terms of empirical first order inter-relationship.

The square of multiple correlation called the 'coefficient of multiple determination' has been used for comparing the proportion of variance accounted for, by two different sets of variables, *i.e.*, personality and organizational climate variables in predicting job performance. In this analysis an attempt has been made to estimate the net effect of a set of predictors and also their joint effect through other set of predictors. Method is referred to as the 'explained variance decomposition analysis' (Mukherjee 1977). Another such analysis has been attempted with job satisfaction as a criterion variable. A comparison of these two variance decomposition analyses throw light on whether same set of predictors can forcast job performance as well as job satisfaction.

Discriminant function analysis determines the weight to be given to each of the original measurements in order that the resulting composite score will have maximum utility in distinguishing between the members of two groups (Overall and Klett 1972). In this study discriminant analysis of the two groups (for good and poor job performers groups) has been computed for personality background and attitudinal variables.

Factor analysis is a powerful method of statistical analysis that aims at explaining relationship among numerous variables in terms of a relatively few underlying factor variates. Factor scores are composite variables that represent the status of factor-dimensions. The organizational climate questionnaire and job performance criteria have been separately processed for intercorrelation and factor analysis to arrive at the cluster of factors.

Results of the study are reported in Chapter ten,

CHAPTER
NINE

Measurement of Job Performance

EMPLOYEE performance refers to an act of fulfilment of the requirement of a given job, *i.e.*, manner in which employee carries out this job, efficiency at work or accomplishment and discharge of duty. Evaluation of such a behaviour is not an easy task, because what criteria to follow for performance evaluation depends on the total work situation. Moreover, who should be the best judge ? What should he evaluate ? What technique should he use ? All these are important questions in employee performance measurement. Thus, nature of work, dimensions of evaluation, criteria, selection of judge and certain other factors are important in this process.

Normally, one hears statements about any person in terms of good or bad etc., such statements are emphasising the unidimensional nature of performance evaluation. However, recent researches have shown that we need multidimensional evaluation of any performance situation.

Nature of job determines whether one has to take a judgemental criteria or some other standards like production records etc. In earlier years perhaps production records were considered the only criterion for employee performance appraisals. In recent years, however, there is a growing realisation that there are a number of other factors too, which contribute to employee effectiveness. This determines various characteristics which are generally important for being a good worker or, are specifically important to a group of jobs,

The crucial question in this regard is that who should be the judge in this process. All these issues have been discussed below with citations of researches. Based on these arguments employee performance criteria has been developed, which shows productivity and employee behaviour as two composits of this process. This tool has been used for the measurement of job performance in this study.

Multidimensional Nature of Job Performance

Seashore, Indik and Georgopolus (1960) conceptualized the concept as multidimensional.

In their study, Seashore et al (1960) of a delivery service firm, they found support for this. Their data are interpreted as contradicting the validity of "overall job performance" as a unidimensional construct, and as a basis for combining job performance variables into a single measure having general validity. The results also indicate that the use of a single job performance variable as a 'sample' of a set of job performances is not justified without prior determination of inter-relations among different aspects of job performance. The study proposed that, in the absence of a comprehensive theory of job performance which takes into account systems of casual and conditioning variables, the measurement and use of job performance criterion variables will remain at primitive stage.

Morrisey (1972) suggested that we must examine a few departments from the traditional practices if we want performance appraisals to be truely effective. He suggested that relationship of objective and subjective measures in appraisals must be considered but he agrees that objective measures are not easy to establish in all situations. The approach, according to him, should be tailor made rather than universal, and it should be a performance appraisal rather than the all purpose evaluation.

Many measures are used by the industrial psychologists for measurement of job performance, and validity of any one of the measures often depends upon the specific set of circumstances under which a particular measure has been evolved and used. Blum and Naylor (1968) suggested rate of work, quality of work, accidents and breakage, dollars earned, job knowledge, job tenure, absenteeism, rate of advancement etc., as measures of job performance. One might, logically, expect production data to be the most frequently used criterion in industrial settings. Interestingly enough, this does not appear to be the case. Schultz and Siegal (1960) point out that production records have been used far less extensively than one would expect and they conclude that such criteria are probably most useful for routine jobs like mass production of items.

Some of the best data on production criteria have been provided by Rothe and his co-workers (1958, 1959, 1951, 1961). Their data offer ample proof that job performance as measured by production data also varies with time. In these studies the values of Correlation coefficients on the reliability of production data ranged from .05 to .85. Ghisselli and Haire (1960) found the correlation for production data between weekly time periods to be considerably higher for adjacent weeks than for weeks widely separated

Often it is easier to acquire information about a person's job behaviour that is not in terms of a production figure but personal data like number of times he is late, accidents and grievances. In using such measures there is often the implicit assumption that they are related to production performance in some manner i.e., the tardy workers are those who will produce less. But relationship between such personal data and actual production is very low (Blum and Naylor 1968). It is suggested that relevant criteria be considered in their own right, rather than a simple substitute for productivity. Baumgartle and Sobol (1959) demonstrated a relationship between job absenteeism, personal history and organization characteristics. Similarly, Argyle, Gardner and Cloffi (1958) used both absenteeism and turnover measure in addition to productivity as criteria for job performance.

In a survey of the articles from Journal of Applied Psychology for the period 1960-1965, Blum and Naylor (1968) report that there is a frequent use in industry of judgemental criteria. The results indicate that 46% used judgemental criteria, 26% production criteria, 18% personal criteria and 24% no criteria. Some of the studies used multiple criteria as well.

While the use of multiple criteria in studies of individual performance are becoming more popular, (Seashore, Indik, Georgopoulos 1960), it is not being used extensively. Kelly (1968) from an analysis of 32 Criterion variables concluded that criterion relationship are variables in size, and that most of the common variance is recounted for by five factors. Therefore, it is not reasonable to take one measure as representing the total performance or to combine the measure in any simple way.

Format and the choice of the rater

Ruderman (1967) defines employee merit rating as a part of a formal systematic technique under which an employee or his performance is judged against some set of measurement standards. These standards may be qualitative, quantitative, relative or purely judgemental. Choice of the format and rater depends on the intended purpose of performance appraisal. Ruderman further suggests, it is possible that one or a combination of the following raters may give their judgement. They are the immediate manager, other managers who are similar with the job, a higher level manager, an industrial relations specialist, employee's peers, the employee himself and his subordinate. Ruderman further views that, in most cases, the individual's immediate manager is in the best position to know the employee and his work. Research by Whitla and Tirrell (1953) indicate, that the best job of rating is done by the level of supervision closest to those being rated. It is emphasised that merit rating for the purpose of improving individual performance may have value in having self-appraisals. Ratings by subordinates find their chief usefulness in selection for promotions.

On the design of performance rating programmes, it is frequently recognised that there may be drawbacks to placing the entire burden on one manager. A higher level manager than the individual's immediate managers may also be required in the appraisals. This review is extended to help in achieving reasonable consistency between the raters and will eliminate any gross misratings.

Shrode and Voich (1974) suggest that qualitative performance standards may be appropriate when it is difficult to quantify the results expected from certain tasks explicitly. The different measure of job performance can be classified into two broad categories i.e., subjective and objective, the former being in the form of rating the employee's efficiency by supervisors, mates or subordinates and latter by having a count of the work unit produced, accidents etc. Merit rating is simply a systematic way for a supervisor to record his judgment about the job performance of an employee. Types of rating methods which are employed to appraise the personal efficiency are graphic rating methods, rating scales, paired comparison, ranking, forced choice, forced distribution, checklist and critical incidence technique. The critical incidence technique is based upon rating of behaviours in real life situations. In recent years the measure of personnel appraisal, which traditionally involved an overall rating by the superiors, have been subject to considerable criticism, but the superiors assessment of the subordinates, is still the most common and frequent measure of job performance (Vroom 1969, Guion 1965). Lawler (1967) assessed the executive performance by the multitrait-multirater method. Method involved self-rating of the managers, peer ratings, subordinates, ratings and superior ratings on a number of clearly defined traits, thus making it possible to determine the validity of the ratings and clearly understand the meaning of the traits.

Levinson (1970) pointed out some of the potential weaknesses in the managing by objective process as it relates to performance appraisal. According to him every organization is a social system, a network of interpersonal relationships. A man may do an excellent job by objective standards of measurement, but may fail miserably as a partner, subordinate, superior or colleague. It is a common place that more people fail to be promoted for personal reasons than for technical inadequacy.

He stressed that we must consider the human element which is not measurable in an objective sense.

Morrisey (1972) made a very important observation in this regard. Every performance appraisal, according to him, needs to have some subjective analysis of those performance factors that do not readily lend themselves to objective measurement. However, this subjective analysis must be directed toward that the employee does rather than what he is. Furthermore, judgments arrived at in this manner must be valid or meaningful. Therefore, relationship between objective and subjective measures, is not an either-or-situation. The basis of evaluation must be made as objective as possible with any subjective judgment, based on objective observations, and attention must be directed to performance rather than personality. The specific approach and the appraisal instrument must be tailored to the requirement of the organisation or the user as a gauge of effective performance.

Procedure

A close analysis of the literature related to job performance measurement research indicates that we can isolate three parametres for the measurement of job performance.

(*a*) Characteristics or qualities to be appraised.

(*b*) Choice of the appraiser, i.e., immediate superior peers or subordinates.

(*c*) The choice of the measure.

Bollows (1954) has listed a number of characteristics which are necessary and desirable in a criterion. The criterion according to him should be, realistic, reliable, representative, related to other criteria, acceptable to job analyst and management, consistent from one situation to another and predictable. He further points out that it should be inexpensive, understandable, relevant, measurable, bias free and discriminating.

Item Selection and Reduction

Manager's opinion and characteristics of job performance reported in aforesaid literature, helped in preparing a list of the characteristics of the skilled workers in Indian industries to be appraised. Agreements between the views of managers and the empirical findings pertaining to the criteria of employee merit ratings were noted. A list of the characteristics, was prepared with items like—errors,—accidents,—absences,—quality of work, —quantity of work, —initiative, - co-operativeness, —sociability, —obedience, —sincerity, —job knowledge, —interest in work, —dependability, —appearance and—originality. In order to arrive at a more precise, discriminating and valid index of job performance with the time available for rating by the raters, the following procedure was followed. For arriving at a few most important variables which should be the components of performance appraisal, 21 managers from reputed industrial undertakings from public and private industries were consulted. Most of them were of the view that although the number of variables accounting for the overall job performance of the worker may be several, it will not be practicable to get such a huge data from supervisors and managers. They argued that at the most, four most important variables should be taken into account out of the list of variables which was gathered from various sources. Managers were to check list, five variables which they thought to be most important components of the job performance of skilled workers. All the managers agreed on quality of work done, quantity of work done and 20 managers agreed on obedience and behaviour towards supervisors. They emphasised that at the skilled workers level no compromise can be made regarding these variables. Further, nine managers agreed to co-operativeness and eight managers agreed to initiative as important job performance components. This shortlisting of variables in order of preference were listed as productivity (quality of work + quantity of work), co-operativeness, obedience and behaviour towards supervisors and initiative. Other variables though reflecting on job performance, were viewed as less important. Thus, content validity of these components of job performance was established, and a realistic and representative criterion acceptable to managements was prepared.

As suggested by Ruderman (1967) and Whitla and Tirrell (1953), it was decided to take ratings from immediate supervisors and managers. This also helped in establishing an estimate of reliability and validity of the ratings. Lawler (1967) has used multitrait-multirater matrix method in job performance to establish the validity. This choice of raters was also supported by managers.

The yard stick for the measurement was a rating scale (Guilford 1971) of five points. Each characteristic was clearly defined. Managers and immediate supervisors were to rate each worker on this five point format which showed degrees such as very good, good, average, poor and very poor. These were scored as five for 'very good', four for 'good', three for 'average', two for 'poor' and one for 'very poor' performance.

Judges (supervisors and managers) were requested not to consult each other. They were further made aware of the errors, they are likely to commit in rating the employees. Moon and Hariton (1958) and Lanham (1955) have indicated that managers with training before rating did a better job at performance appraisals. In the rating form, an instruction paragraph was included (Appendix B) indicating the effects of aforesaid errors likely to creep into their judgements.

In addition to this data, objective production records were also obtained from mass producing units. Table IX.1 presents product moment correlations between different items of job performance criteria for two judges.

TABLE IX.1

Inter-Correlations Between Job Performance Items for Total Sample for Two Judges

	1	2	3	4	
1. Productivity	—	.458	.568	.554	RATER I
2. Co-operation		—	.693	.570	
3. Obedience and behaviour with Supervisors			—	.343	
4. Initiative				—	
1. Productivity	—	.615	.418	.746	RATER II
2. Co-operation		—	.825	.370	
3. Obedience			—	.535	
4. Initiative				—	

N=397

All the correlations are significant above .01 level.

Correlations between productivity ratings and production records available for two mass producing units were computed to be .89 (N=56). This highly significant correlation gives further weightage to the validity of productivity data.

Factor analysis

Further correlation matrix of all the eight variables (Two judges) was factor analysed to arrive at smaller factor variates and to see whether job performance is a unidimensional concept.

Studies by Turner (1960), Dugan (1960), Taylor, Smith, Ghiselin and Ellison (1961), Seashore, Andrik and Georgopoulos (1960) have also used factor analysis in determining their criteria of job

TABLE IX.2

Multi traits—Raters Matrix

Charact-eristics	*Raters*	*Product-ivity*	*Co-operative-ness*	*Obedience and behaviour*	*Initiat-ive*
		1			
1. Productivity	I	.859	.458	.568	.554
	II	1			
			1		
2. Co-operative-					
ness	I	.615	.821	.693	.570
	II		1		
				1	
3. Obedience	I				
and		.418	.825	.832	.343
Behaviour	II				
				1	
					1
4. Initiative	I	.746	.370	.535	.801
	II			1	

Table IX.2 presents the multitrait—multi rater matrix.

performance. They have generally argued that job performance is not a unidimensional concept.

Principal components factor analysis method was applied to the inter correlation matrix of eight variables (combined for two judges) and results were rotated using Kaiser's (1958) varimax criterion. Two factor solution emerged. Results of unrotated and rotated factor analyses are presented in table IX.3 and table IX.4 respectively.

Items with loading above .5 on a particular factor were considered for interpretation from varimax rotated results of factor analysis.

TABLE IX.3

Unrotated Factor Matrix for Eight Items of Job Performance Scale for Total Sample (N=397)

Item No.	*Factors* 1	2
1.	.775	.386
2.	.799	.391
3.	.770	.447
4.	.689	.498
5.	.840	.329
6.	.861	.315
7.	.848	.386
8.	.819	.411
Eigen Value	5.145	1.274
Percentage of Trace	64.312	15.930

TABLE IX.4

Varimax Rotated Factor Loadings for Eight Items of Job Performance Scale. For Total Sample (N=397)

Item No.	*Factors* 1	2	h^2
1	.296	.814	75.019
2	.848	.267	79.060
3	.867	.206	79.361
4	.157	.836	72.293
5	.383	.817	81.355
6	.841	.305	84.099
7	.881	.305	86.840
8	.310	.862	83.914
Percentage of Variation	41.356	38.887	

Factor I

It is observed that item numbers 2, 3, 6 and 7 are loading high on factor I. These items and their factor loadings are as follows :

.848	Co-operativeness
.867	Behaviour towards superiors and obedience—I
.841	Co-operativeness—II
.881	Behaviour towards superiors—II

All these items reflect on personality based job linked behaviour. Job performance as an index of appraised behaviour is the result of integrated functioning of individual. This approach according to Mackinney (1967) is needed for appraisals in every step of performance ladder. This factor was interpreted as job performance (behavioural factor). Behavioural factors mean that certain uniformities can be detected running through an individual's behaviour which typically seem to have obvious connection with the capacity to work, and affect the mode of dealing with others and environment generally (Welford 1968). Thus these become components of successful accomplishment of the job.

Factor II

.814	Productivity I.
.836	Initiative I.
.817	Productivity II.
.862	Initiative II.

Item numbers 1, 4, 5 and 8 are showing high loadings on factor II in the varimax rotated factor analysis presented above. All these items refer to actual production of the goods in industries in terms of productivity and initiative. This factor is referred to as job performance (productivity factor). Results of factor analysis further support the ratings of two raters, i.e., supervisors and managers in terms of factorial validity.

Data reflect that the job performance is not an unidimensional concept. Therefore, it is necessary to assess the total situation in which job linked behaviour occurs.

Scoring

For the final analysis of the factors related to job performance, components of each job performance factors were added up to give two indices of different dimensions of job performance. These two dimensions are used separately (in productivity analysis) as well as a total score was obtained by adding up all these item scores, as a composite job performance score which was used for analysis.

CHAPTER
TEN

Discussion of Results

JOB PERFORMANCE AND INTELLIGENCE

Hypothesis I

(*i*) This hypothesis states that intelligence of the worker is related to his job performance.

Correlation coefficients between intelligence and job performance for various groups of samples in the present investigation are as follows :

TABLE X.1

Samples	*r between job performance and intelligence*
Public sector (N=139)	.002
Private sector (N=258)	.062
Males (N=353)	.054
Females (N=44)	—.09

It is observed that all the correlation coefficients table X.1 which are ranging between .002 to .09, are very low and statistically not significant denoting almost no relationship between these two variables.

(*ii*) Workers in very good and very poor job performance groups and their intelligence.

For the test of this part of the hypothesis, the results of the analysis of two extreme groups of good and poor job performers with regard to intelligence are considered which are as follows :

TABLE X.2

Upper Mean (N=35)	76.062
Lower Mean (N=30)	66.094
Mean Difference	9.968
't'	.62

This shows that the value of 't' is too low and not significant, confirming that even the extreme groups of job performers do not differ in their intelligence in the sample investigated. Thus, this hypothesis could not be supported.

French (1957) studied joint effects of intelligence and achievement motivation on problem solving performance of airmen. He found that performance of those having high achievement motivation, was positively related to intelligence. However, there was no relationship between performance and intelligence for those low in motivation.

In this investigation, a minimum level of technical skill of the worker has been kept constant by including only skilled workers with industrial training diploma. Generally, persons with very low intelligence are not likely to pass the diploma and therefore, might not have been present in the sample studied. It may be observed that the range of the score on the test of intelligence, is from 55 to 105 with only a few cases below a score of 65 and above 95 and the mean is 78.164. The sample seems to be quite homogeneous with regard to intelligence. This factor of homogeneity might have contributed to lack of relationship between the level of intelligence and job performance.

JOB PERFORMANCE AND BACKGROUND VARIABLES

Hypothesis II

(*i*) This hypothesis states that certain background variables like age, experience, tenure, and SES, are related to the level of job performance, Results of these analyses are presented in Table X.3,

TABLE X.3

Intercorrelations between Job Performance and Background Variables (N=397)

Variables	*r*
Age	—.050
Marital Status	—.044
Experience	—.028
Length of present tenure	.025
SES	.127*
Income	.108*

*P<.05

Intercorrelations indicate that only socio-economic status (r=.127) and income (r=.108) are related to the level of job performance. These correlations are significant at 5% level of significance. Variables like age, marital status, experience and tenure in the present organisation do not seem to have any relationship with the level of job performance. The results indicate that those in higher socio-economic status and with more income are better at job performance.

(*ii*) Relationships between background variables and the level of job performance (male and female employees).

Product-moment correlations are presented in Table X.4.

TABLE X.4

Product-moment Correlations between Background Variables and the level of Job Performance for Male and Female Workers

Variables	*r for male workers (N=353)*	*r for female workers (N=44)*
Age	—.031	—.180
Marital Status	—.061	.078
Experience	—.026	—.036
Present tenure	.037	—.056
SES	.137*	.061
Income	.106*	.123

*P<.05

**P<.01

Pattern of correlations indicate that none of the correlations are statistically significant for female employees, whereas in case of males, income and SES are significant at 5% level of significance.

(*iii*) Patterns of correlations between background variables and the level of job performance (for public and private sector employees) correlations are presented in Table X.5.

TABLE X.5

Correlations between Background Variables and the level of Job Performance for Two Samples of Fublic and Private Industries

Variables	*Public Sector* *r (N=139)*	*Private Sector* *r (N=258)*
Age	—.087	—.125*
Marital Status	—.137	—.001
Experience	.002	—.046
Length of present tenure	.016	.042
SES	.154	.123*
Income	.164*	.082

*P<.05

**P<.01

It is observed that the pattern of correlations are generally same except in case of age, SES and income. There is a significant relationship of income and the level of job performance in case of public sector employees. In case of private sector workers, level of job performance has a significant relationship with age and SES. Data suggest that those who are in high socio-economic level and have more income (as these variables are likely to be interdependent) perform better at the job. Perhaps the employees who are placed in better economic conditions pay relatively less attention to financial gains and look for higher need satisfaction in their job. This might have led to their better performance. Age shows a negative significant relationship with job performance in case of private sector workers. This indicates that the younger the employee, better he performs in private industry. However, in public sector industries there is a positive trend.

(*iv*) Workers in very good and very poor job performance groups and their background variables, a two group discriminant analysis was applied to the workers below 25th percentile and above 75th percentile on job performance scale. Results are presented in Table X.6

TABLE X.6

Discriminant Analysis of Background Characteristics of Very Good and Very Poor Job Performance

Variables	*Lower mean*	*Upper mean*	*Mean Difference*	*Discriminant function coefficient*	*SDF Weights*
Age	26.929	27.215	—.286	.009	.045
Marital Status	1.312	1.231	—.081	1.364	.644
Experience	6.219	7.369	1.150	.047	.223
Length of present Tenure	4.250	6 369	2.119	.108	.456
SES	38.531	44.354	5.823	.048	.517
Income	2.156	2.738	.582	1.299	.894
'F' ratio=75.186					

$N_1 = 30$
$N_2 = 35$

In the discriminant function analysis, high discriminant function coefficients obtained are for marital status and income. In a study by Taylor (1975), age was found to influence performance in decision making.

Sinha and Agrawal (1971) have also reported that older workers have higher job motivation. In case of women workers, there is a perceptible negative relationship with age indicating that younger women workers are better at job performance.

Generally, results are suggestive of the idea that background characteristics do not show much influence on the level of job performance except with regard to SES and income.

JOB PERFORMANCE AND ATTITUDES

Hypothesis III

(*i*) Attitudes of the workers towards organization are related to their level of job performance.

TABLE X.7

Product Moment Correlations between Job Attitudes and Job Performance

Attitudes	*r*
Job satisfaction reported	—.177*
Perception of self development opportunities	—.106*
Feeling of belongingness (Espirit, Warmth)	—.067
Attitude towards working conditions	.086
Attitude towards supervision	—.035
Attitude towards financial benefits	—.019
Attitude towards employment security	—.055
Attitude towards interaction & communication opportunities	.188**
Attitude towards self esteem and consideration	.118*

**P<.01 N=397

*P<.05

It is observed from table X.7 that attitudes denoting perception of self-development opportunities (r = —.106) self esteem and consideration perception (r = .118) and communication opportunities (r = .188) show some relationship with the level of job performance. Relationship is closest in case of interaction and communication opportunities perceived within the organization, which is significant at .01 level. Perception of self development opportunity shows a negative relationship indicating that those who are good performers do not perceive the fulfilment of self-development needs. Attitude towards self esteem and consideration is positively related to the level of job performance, significance level being .05. Job satisfaction shows a relationship of r = —.177 with the level of job performance. Though all the relationships are not very high, they generally seem to suggest support for Herzberg et al's (1959) theory that only the higher order needs, are the motivating factors. There seems to be no relationship between the level of job performance and feeling of belongingness, working conditions, supervision financial benefits, and employment security, all perceived within the organisation. Brayfield and Crockett (1955) have concluded that there is little evidence of any simple or appreciable relationship between employee attitude and their job performance.

(*ii*) Pattern of correlations between their attitudes and the level of job performance in case of male and female workers.

TABLE X.8

Correlations between Level of Job Performance and Attitudes for Male and Female Samples

Attitudes	*Males* (*N=353*)	*Females* (*N=44*)
Job satisfaction reported	.089	—.298*
Perception of self development opportunities	—.100	—.145
Feeling of belongingness (Espirit)	—.093	.118
Attitude towards working conditions	.102	—.017
Attitude towards supervision	—.010	—.200
Attitude towards financial benefits	—.037	.094
Attitude towards employment security	.071	—.057
Attitude towards interaction & communication opportunities	.172**	.299*
Attitude towards self esteem & consideration	.172**	—.260

** P < .01
* P < .05

It is observed from table X.8 that there is a negative relationship of job performance with the job satisfaction in case of female workers. Male workers show a positive relationship (r=.102) with attitude towards working conditions. Perception of interaction opportunities, has positive correlation with job performance amongst both groups.

Attitude towards self-esteem and consideration shows significant positive relation in case of males, but negative in case of females. Females also show a negative trend towards closeness of supervision, though the value of correlation is not very high. Attitude towards financial benefits, does not show any significant relationship with the level of job performance in both cases.

(*iii*) Workers in public and private sector industries and the relationship between job attitudes and job performance.

TABLE X.9

Correlations between Job Performance and Attitudes for Public and Private Sector

Attitudes	*Public sector*	*Private sector*
Job satisfaction reported	.042	—.190**
Perception of self development opportunities	—.071	—.126*
Feeling of belongingness (Espirit)	—.166*	—.010
Attitude towards working conditions	.121	.070
Attitude towards supervision	.048	—.080
Attitude towards financial benefits	—.134	.040
Attitude towards employment security	.173*	—.004
Attitude towards interaction & communication opportunities	.180*	.195**
Attitude towards self esteem & consideration opportunities	.189*	.081

** P < .01

(N = 139) (N = 258)

* P < .05

It is observed from table X.9 that, in case of private industry workers, reported job satisfaction is negatively related to job performance (r=—.190) where as in case of those in public sector industry, there is no significant correlation.

Correlation of self development opportunities with job performance, in case of workers in private industries is r=—.126, but no significant correlation is found for workers in public sector.

However, workers in public sector show a positive relationship (r=.189) between self-esteem and job performance which is not in case of workers in private industries (r=.081).

Interaction opportunities perceived show positive relationship in both categories though it is weaker in case of public sector.

Pestonjee and Basu (1973) concluded on the basis of a study of Indian executives that both, private and public sector executives have similar job motivations.

Results of this investigation, indicate that there seems to be more clear relationship between workers' job attitude and their level of job performance in case of employees in private industrial set-ups. Porter (1962) found that managers in Government firms are, generally, less satisfied than their counterparts in the private industries. Findings of the present investigation show opposite relationship.

Sinha (1973) analysed 'some problems of public sector organisations' in India. His findings suggest that, generally, managers in public and private sector industries in India are quite comparable in their need, structure and values. It is observed that contextual factors or hygiene factors concern them more. However, on the basis of the comparisons of the mean scores of managers in two reputed private and public sector industries, he emphasised that private industries have promoted conditions such as sense of responsibility, better social relations, initiative and better working conditions, hence, a better organisational climate. He pointed out that managers in public sector also feel that their initiative and hard work are not rewarded. In the present investigation, results showing high relationship between internality in locus of control and the level of job performance are also suggestive such trend. However, gap in motivation patterns of the employees in these two sectors, does not seem to be very wide in the present investigation.

(*iv*) Good and poor performers and their attitudes towards organisational climate. To analyse the difference in attitudes, a two group discriminant function analysis was applied. Workers, who were below 25th percentile and above 75th percentile in the job performance scores were included in the analysis. Table X.10 shows lower (low performers) and upper groups means (high performer). F, ratio is calculated to be 17.82 which is significant at .01 level. Highest discriminant function coefficient is obtained for job satisfaction.

The analysis indicates that, in case of reported feeling of job satisfaction, the two groups are discriminating maximum, with discriminant function coefficient being 1.708.

JOB PERFORMANCE AND ORGANISATIONAL CLIMATE

Hypothesis IV

(*i*) Perception of organisational climate as a whole and the level of job performance of the workers.

TABLE X.10

Discriminant Function Analysis of Attitudes of Good and Poor Performers

Attitudes	*Lower mean (N=30)*	*Upper mean (N=35)*	*Differ-ence*	*Discriminant function co-efficients*
Job satisfaction reported	1.594	1.431	—.163	1.708
Perception of organisational climate	126.844	126.06	—.784	—.001
Perception of self-developed opportunities	35.687	33.000	—2.687	—.087
Feeling of belongingness (Espirit etc.)	34.406	32.646	—1.760	—.045
Attitude towards working conditions	33.687	35.262	1.570	.040
Attitude towards supervision	3.250	3.231	—.019	—.004
Attitude towards financial benefits	3,531	3.631	.100	.023
Attitude towards interaction & communication opportunities	3.250	4.062	.812	.086
Attitude towards employment security	2.625	2.892	.267	.056
Attitude towards self-esteem & consideration opportunities	3.219	3.662	.443	.082

F ratio=17.82

As revealed from the present analysis, correlation coefficients between global perception of organisational climate and job performance for various samples are as follows :

Public sector (N = 139)	—.019
Private sector (N = 258)	—.056

These correlations are low and statistically not significant. However, the trend shows a negative relationship though very weak. Results suggest that global perception of the organisational climate does not, in any way, influence the job performance. Earlier, in hypothesis III, it was observed that some of the attitudes, included in the organisational climate individually seem to have a significant relationship with job performance.

(*iv*) Workers in very good and very poor performance groups and their perception of the climate of the organisation. Results, of a two group analysis are as follows :

Lower group Mean (N=30)	126.340
Upper group Mean (N=35)	126.062
Mean difference	—.782
't'	.29

The value of 't' which is .29, is not significant. This suggests that the two groups do not differ significantly as regards to their global perception of organisational climate.

Rao and Chattopadhyay (1974) attempted to study the relationship between productivity and organisational climate in small industries in India. They also found these variables to be unrelated.

Research, involving organisational climate and job performance is further complicated by studies which arrives at opposite conclusions. Friedlander and Greenberg (1971) showed that effective organisational behaviour was associated with a supportive climate. Meglino (1976) suggested that an evaluative climate can enhance performance at well learned tasks while retarding performance at poorly learned tasks. Using this relationship, he suggested that series of research studies, which, at first, seem unrelated or even contradictory, can be connected in a unified thread. He, however, felt that the concept of organisational climate, as related to job performance has not been fully explored.

The present investigation was conducted to find the relationship between these two variables amongst well trained skilled workers, but no clear relationship could be established. However, when these attitudes (different factors of OCQI) were correlated independently, they showed some relationship with the job performance as revealed by the explanation of hypothesis III.

JOB PERFORMANCE AND PERSONALITY VARIABLES

Hypothesis V

(*i*) This hypothesis states that certain personality variables like level of occupational aspiration, locus of control and values are related to the level of job performance of the industrial workers.

To study these relationships, correlation coefficients were computed. These correlation, coefficients are presented in table X.11.

TABLE X.11

Correlations between the Level of Job Performance and Certain Personality Variables

Variables	*r with job performance*
Locus of control	.189**
Level of occupational aspiration	.465**
Religious value	—.125*
Aesthetic value	.036
Political value	—.019
Economic value	.004
Social value	.012
Theoretical value	.166**

N=397 **$P<.01$
*$P<.05$

The table reveals that workers, who show higher internal locus of control have a significant relationship with job performance (r=.189), *i.e.*, those workers who believe in their efforts rather than fate, are better performers on the job.

Broedling (1975) reported that internal locus of control was related to work motivation. Andrisoni and Nestel (1976) also provided considerable support to the hypothesis that success at work enhances expectancy of internal controls.

Level, of occupational aspirations has a highly significant positive correlation with job performance (r=.465). Workers who aspire to become higher executives such as Chief Engineers and Managers of the industries, are better job performers. This indicates that they perform better as they want to achieve their goals.

Value pattern indicates that workers, who are high in theoretical value (r=.166) and low in religious value (r=.125) have better performance at the job. Persons, with high theoretical value behave in the theoretically proper way, and might be performing better as a matter of duty. Those who are high in religious value, show a significantly negative relationship with job performance. This indicates that who have religious bent of mind, might be expecting the success in life by worship of God and not by their efforts. This result is consistent with the finding that high internals, in locus of control are also good job performers. Generally, all other values *i.e.*, political (—.019), social (.012), aesthetic (.036) and the economic value (.004) do not show any significant relationship with job performance.

This hypothesis states that male and female workers show different patterns of relationships between certain personality variables and the level of job performance. Table X.12 presents correlation coefficients between these variables.

TABLE X.12

Correlations between Personality Variables and Job Performance of Male and Female Workers

Variables	*Males (N=353)*	*Females (N=44)*
Locus of control	.223**	—.048
Level of occupational aspiration	.468**	.435**
Religious Value	—.150**	.074
Aesthetic Value	.057	—.245
Political Value	—.005	—.113
Theoretical Value	.135*	.385*
Economic Value	.031	—.183
Social Value	.029	.310

*P$<$.05

**P$<$.01

Pattern of correlations suggests that there is a high positive relationship between internal locus of control and the level of job performance in case of male employees (r=.203), whereas females do not show any significant relationship between these two variables.

The findings are consistent with some reported researches. Nowicki (1973) reported that externality was associated with achievement for females (r=.39, N=.26) while internality was related to achievement for males (r=—.50, N=22). Noditch and Demaio (1975) in a study of school performance and locus of control, also indicated similar results.

Level, of occupational aspirations is showing high positive correlation with the level of job performance. In case of male workers, relationship seems to be slightly higher (r=.468) than female workers (r=.435). Religious value has a significant negative correlation with the job performance (r=.140) in case of male workers, but not in case of females. Theoretical value shows a high correlation with the level of job performance in case of women workers (r=.385). Male workers also show a positive relationship of this variable with job performance (r=.138). Other values do not seem to have obvious relationship with the level of job performance.

(*iii*) The relationship between certain personality variables and the level of job performance for public and private industry workers. Table X.13 presents the correlations. It is observed that, though both, public and private sector workers show a significant positive correlation between the level of occupational aspiration and job performance, the relationship is much higher, and in case of workers in private industry. Workers in public undertakings do not show any relationship of job performance with internal locus of control, whereas private sector workers show a high correlation (r=.304).

This again confirms the earlier finding that the workers in public sector industries feel that the advancement in career can not be much influenced by their efforts as seniority and other factors still dominate. Value pattern also shows more effect amongst workers in private sector than in public sector industries. Theoretical value shows a positive relationship (r=.219) and religious value shows a significant negative relationship (r=—.141) with the level of job performance in case of private sector employees.

Table X.13 indicates that skilled workers, both in public and private sector industries show significant correlation between personality variables and job performance. But the relationship is much closer in case of private sector employees.

TABLE X.13

Correlations between Job Performance and Personality Variables in Public and Private Sector Industries

Variables	*Public Sector* (*N=139*)	*Private Sector* (*N=258*)
Level of Occupational Aspiration	.372**	.525**
Locus of Control	.048	.304**
Theoretical Value	.086	.219*+
Religious Value	—.100	—.141*
Aesthetic Value	—.067	.089
Social Value	—.074	.058
Political Value	—.043	—.009
Economic Value	.095	—.081

**P<.01

*P<.05

(*iv*) Workers in very good and very poor job performance groups and their value patterns, table X.14 presents results of discriminant analysis for six value dimensions. It is seen that maximum difference, in means of the two groups is in the case of theoretical value *i.e.*, 3,872. This value discriminates highly between the two extreme groups with highest discriminant function coefficient (.104). F ratio is calculated to be 94.80 which is significant at 1% level.

TABLE X.14

Discriminant Analysis of Values of Very Good and Very Poor Job Performers

Values	*Lower group means*	*Upper group means*	*Mean difference*	*Discriminant function coefficient*
Religious Value	31.062	27.600	—3.462	—.042
Aesthetic Value	37.781	38.969	1.188	.024
Political Value	40.062	38.123	—1.939	—.040
Economic Value	45.781	44.015	—1.766	—.033
Social Value	41.250	43.323	2.073	.050
Theoretical Value	46.312	50.185	3.872	.104

F ratio=94 80 $N_1=30$, $N_2=35$

Findings indicate that personality characteristics, of the workers contribute to his level of job performance. Saunders and Stanton (1976) attempted to study the pattern of relationship between personality traits and performance styles. Using cannonical correlations, authors also concluded that psychological variables play important role in the success of goal attainment.

Hypothesis VI

(*i*) Predicting employee productivity through personality variables as intervening variables between attitudes and job productivity.

Regression analysis was used to test the hypothesis.

A regression model of productivity was tested for perception of need satisfaction in job situation. Another regression was obtained for personality variables like locus of control, occupational aspiration and theoretical value. A third regression analysis was carried out by combining all the above variables. Results of regression analyses are tabulated in tables X. 15, 16 and 17, and percentages of variations in table X.18.

It is observed from table X.18 that variance explained by personality variables, is 25.39% whereas job situation variables are accounting only for 8.42% of variance. Taken together, these variables, in regressions analysis, account for 31.45% of variance. Thus, personality is accounting for 23.03% and job situation is accounting for 6.05% of a variance in the sample investigated.

TABLE X.15

Regression Analysis of Perceptual Variables Denoting Higher Need Satisfaction as Predictors of Productivity

Variables	*Multiple R*	R^2	*B*	*Beta weight*	*St. error of B*	*F. ratio*
Perception of self development opportunities	.052	.002	.053	.246	.013	17.095
Interaction opportunities perceived	.246	.060	.269	.241	.059	20.525
Consideration opportunities perceived	.290	.084	.188	.182	.059	10.131

Results indicate that higher order need perception variables as well as personality variables appear to function more clearly as independent determinants of productivity than as intervening variables.

TABLE X.16

Regression Analysis of some Personality and Job Situation Variables as Predictors of Productivity

Variables	*Multiple R*	R^2	*B*	*Beta weight*	*St. Error of B*	*F. ratio*
Perception of self development opportunity	.052	.002	.051	233	.011	19.938
Locus of control	.217	.047	.019	.085	.010	3.829
Occupational aspiration	.487	.237	.647	.415	.067	92.509
Theoretical value	.508	.258	.026	.146	.007	11.632
Introduction opportunity	.542	.294	.210	.188	.051	16.399
Consideration opportunity	.560	.314	.174	.168	.051	11.343

TABLE X.17

Percentages and Proportions of Variations Explained by Personality and Perceptual Job Situation Variables in Predicting Productivity

Source of variation	*Proportion of variance explained*	*Variation in percent*
Personality (Locus of control (I), occupational aspiration & theoretical value)	.25392	25.39
Perceptual job situation variables	.0842	8.42
Both personality and job situation perception	.31447	31.45
Personality alone	.23027	23.03
Job situation alone	.06045	6.05
Personality through perception	.02365	2.36

PRODUCTIVITY AND JOB SATISFACTION

Hypothesis VIII

(*i*) Relationship between job satisfaction and productivity and sets of variables predicting them.

In the present investigation, correlations between reported job satisfaction and job performance range between .042 to —.298 as revealed from tables in hypothesis III. The relationships for various samples are as follows.

	'*r*'
Male sample (N=353)	—.089
Female sample (N=44)	—.298*
Public sector (N=139)	.042
Private sector (N=258)	—.190**

Hackman and Lawler (1971) report a positive correlation between job motivation, satisfaction and performance only for employees reporting satisfaction of higher order needs, *i.e.*, need for accomplishment, growth, challenge and participation.

Vroom (1964) analysed data from 20 studies exploring relationship between job performance and job satisfaction and pointed out that the value of correlations, coefficients ranged

TABLE X.18

Regression Analysis of Personality Variables as Predictors of Job Satisfaction

Variables	*Multiple R*	R^2	*B*	*Beta weight*	*St. error of B*	*F. ratio*
Level of Occupational Aspiration	.113	.012	.008	.141	.003	7.553
Locus of Control	.125	.015	.006	.065	.005	1.645
Religious Value	.148	.021	.006	.107	.002	4.214
Aesthetic Value	.163	.026	—.005	—.072	.004	1.685
Political Value	.164	.027	.003	.041	.004	.535
Economic Value	.171	.029	.004	.069	.003	1.611
Social Value	.214	.046	.011	—.144	.004	6.950
Theoretical Value	.219	048	.003	.047	.004	.728

between .86 to −.31. Likert (1961) has suggested that the relationship, between satisfaction and performance becomes more positive as the level of skill required by the job increases.

Regression analysis was applied to find out the proportions of variance accounted for, by personality variables and job situation variables in predicting job satisfaction. Table X.18 presents the results of analysis for personality factors in predicting job satisfaction. These factors are accounting for 4.8% of variance in predicting job satisfaction.

TABLE X.19

Regression Analysis of Job Situation Attitudes as Predictors of Job Satisfaction

Variables	*Multiple R*	R^2	*B*	*Beta weight*	*St. error of B*	*F. ratio*
Organisational climate	.468	.219	.004	.228	.001	15.720
Perception of Self actualising opportunities	.510	.260	.018	.191	.006	8.383
Feeling of belongingness	.519	.269	.004	.049	.005	.607
Attitude towards work condition	.542	.293	.011	.140	.004	5.558
Attitude towards close supervision	.552	.305	.045	.115	.016	7.035
Attitude to financial benefit	.557	.310	.037	.093	.023	2.688
Employment security perceived	.557	.310	—.001	—.002	.018	0.004
Interacting opportunities perceived	.558	.312	—.019	—.039	.023	0.697
Contributing opportunities perceived	·560	.314	—.025	—.056	.023	1,214

TABLE X.20

Regression Analysis of Personality Variables as Predictors of Productivity

Variables	*Multiple R*	R^2	*B*	*Beta weight*	*St. error of B*	*F. ratio*
Locus of control	.201	.04	.021	.091	.010	4.129
Level of occupational aspiration	.483	.23	.680	.436	.069	95.411
Theoretical Value	.503	.25	.026	.143	.008	10.559

Table X.19 presents attitudinal factors predicting job satisfaction. These variables, together account for 31.4% of variance explained in prediction of job satisfaction.

Proportions and percentages accounted for by job situation variables and personality variables in prediction of job satisfaction are presented in table X.21.

TABLE X.21

Variables	*Proportion of Variance*	*Percentage of Variance*
Perception of job situation	.31411	31.41
Personality variables	.04 97	4.79
Job situation and personality variables together	.36208	36.20

When compared with prediction of productivity, these variables show a different pattern. Earlier, table X.20 has presented findings on productivity. Proportion and percentages, of variance explained by personality variables and perception of job situation variables in predicting productivity and job satisfaction are as follows ;

TABLE X.22

Variables	*Percentages of variance explained in predicting*	
	Productivity	*Job satisfaction*
Personality variables	25.39%	4.79%
Job situation variables	8.42%	31.41%
Both personality and job situation variables	31.45%	36.20%

PREDICTION OF JOB PERFORMANCE

Hypothesis VIII

To test this hypothesis, that background, personality and attitudinal variables included in the study will predict job performance, a Stepwise Multiple Regression Analysis was performed. This method enables us to separate out the most relevant independent variables from the set studied for prediction.

Table IX.23 a list multiple regression results (stepwise) for background variables, personality variables and attitudes with job performance as the criterion variable. The unstandardised regression coefficients (B), the standard error of the coefficients (SE), the standardised regression coefficients (beta weights), F ratios, and multiple correlations have been computed which are presented in this table. First six predictor variables i.e. occupational aspiration, interaction opportunity, self development opportunity, consideration opportunity, theoretical value have 'F' ratio which is significant at .01 significance level. These variables, though accounting for only about 31.3% of the total variation, are statistically significant at .01 level of confidence in predicting performance.

Variables like locus of control, SES and aesthetic value (negative) are significant at 5% level of significance indicating that these variables can also predict the level of job performance, although to lesser extent. All these 9 variables account for 33.8% of variance. Other types of values, age, intelligence, experience, marital status and attitudes related to working conditions, job security, supervision etc., seem to have negligible predictive capacity. All the 24 variables in equation account for 38.25% of variance,

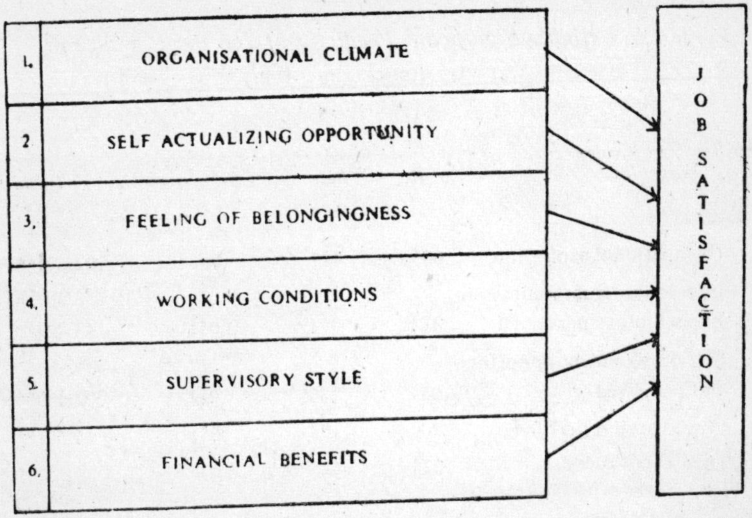

Fig. 10.1 Attitudes Predicting Job Perfoımance (Step-wise regression analysis)

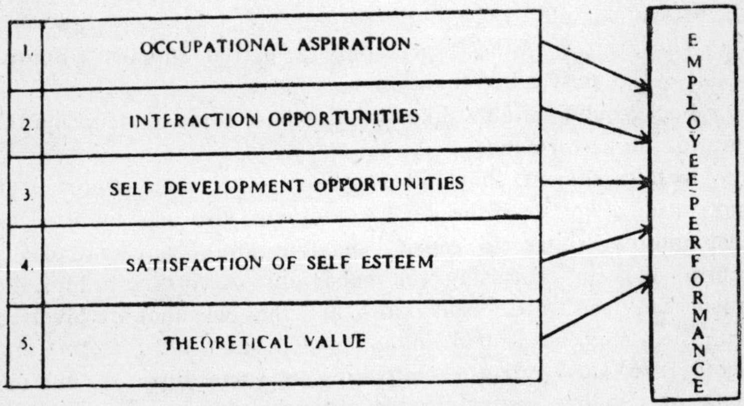

Fig. 10.2 Predictions of Job Performance (Step-wise regression analysis)

TABLE X.23

First Six Highly Significant Predictor of Job Performance in Stepwise Regression Analysis
(N=397)

Variables	*B*	*Beta Weights*	*St. error B*	*F. Ratio*
1. Occupational aspiration	.666	.427	.065	102.671**
2. Interaction-communication opportunities perceived	.191	.171	.051	13.729**
3. Self development opportunities perceived	—.054	—.238	.011	22.439**
4. Consideration perceived	.202	.195	.051	15.551**
5. Theoretical value	.024	.25	.008	8.802**

A review of the analysis shows that variables, such as income and attitude towards financial benefits could not be included in the stepwise regression analysis because the tolerance level or F level was found insufficient for further computation. It seems, these two variables are not important predictors of job performance in the present sample.

Thus, this hypothesis gets only a partial support from the result of the present investigation.

Background variables like SES also have some influence on the level of job performance.

Results suggest that intrinsic factors are most important in motivating a worker at the job. Deci (1976) also has emphasized that internal states do cause behaviour, and cognitions play a central part in energising the behaviour. According to him, the intrinsically motivated behaviours are the ones that are involved with the human need for being competent and self determining. Scott (1976) views intrinsic motivation as some form of internal state presumably distinguishable from the state brought about by the occurrence of reinforcing events, and the important determinants of behaviour.

However, certain factors (in job situation) have also been found to motivate employees. These factors generally, fall in the category of Herzberg's motivators and Maslow's higher order needs,

They also show high valence in motivating an employee in the light of Vroom's model. It is observed that a synthesis of these views, be more successful in prediction of job performance of workers in industries.

Mc. Greger's 'theory Y' and Argyris's theory of organisational behaviour as related to job performance seem to be supported by the results.

The results are suggestive of a cognitive organisation involving worker's values, aspiration and way of viewing the world along with perception of certain job situation factors, predicting job performance. Thus, the model proposed in this investigation gets support from the findings. Goldman (1970) has emphasised similar views in his 'theory of human action'. Action, according to him, flows from desires, beliefs and abilities of the performer.

Pervin (1968) has also stressed that performance and satisfaction result from the interaction of individual and environmental factors. Without combining these aspects, an important component in the understanding of total system of organisational behaviour, will be missing.

CONCLUSIONS OF THE STUDY

Certain personality variables, background and perception of organisational climate have been found to influence the job performance of the workers in the sample studied. Level of occupational aspiration and theoretical value have come out to be most significant personality factors in this regard. Therefore, it is not only sufficient to provide higher wages, better fringe benefits and comfortable environment to the worker for higher job motivation, but much more is required on the psychological front.

Review of the results indicates that same set of variables do not show same pattern of variance in predicting productivity and job satisfaction. Job satisfaction seems to be more influenced by organisational climate variables, whereas productivity seems to be more a function of the personality of the worker.

Locke (1974) concluded that job satisfaction exerts little influence on productivity. It is emphasized that, when these two variables are related at all, the evidence supports an interpretation in favour of productivity as a cause of satisfaction, rather than vice-versa (Greene 1973, Wanous 1974).

All the above findings, of the present investigation suggest that it is a combination of factors internally to employee personality and job situation (related to higher order need fulfilment of the employees) that results in better job performance.

Personality factors generally, show overwhelming influence on the job performance. Among these, factors, such as aspiration for high occupational status, higher theoretical value, lower aesthetic value and internality in locus of control are most significant.

Some job situation factors like perception of consideration, interaction-communication opportunities and lack of self development opportunities within the organisation also seem to contribute significantly to the prediction of job performance.

There are many work situations in industries where neither quantitative assessment of the worker's output, nor estimation of time required to complete the assigned tasks can be made. It has to be left mainly on the worker's initiative, and sincerity, with no effective supervisory control possible. Findings of the present investigation may be of some help specially in such situations. Testing of aforesaid characteristics of the candidates can be an aid to managers while recruitment is done.

In the light of the findings of this study, it is concluded that internal factors, within the worker and within the job opportunities influence the job performance. However, the author feels that larger and longitudinal studies are needed before these findings are finally recommended for policy making.

Limitations of the Study and Scope for Further Research

No research is perfect and always there are points to ponder :

1. The study needs to be done on a larger sample from all types of industries.

2. The organisational climate questionnaire and job performance criteria need to be further refined. Harris (1967) suggests that the given theoretical ambivalence about different methods of factor analysis, it is a sound policy to utilise several methods on any given data set. He advises retaining only those factors commonly identified by each method. These suggestions may be incorporated in further research with larger data and different types of occupational groups.

3. Vroom (1966) suggests that there should be more dynamic correlational studies rather than 'static correlational studies'. Dynamic correlational studies, according to him, are studies in which one looks at the correlations between changes in organisational variables over time, rather than in simply looking at absolute values at one specific moment. Effort should be made to further extend this study in the light of Vroom's suggestions.

4. The study has emphasised personality variables as important factors related to employee job performance in industries. Other types of industrial workers (white collar workers) and other occupational fields may be studied to get more validity.

5. According to Porter (1962), people in different hierarchy level in management, differ in their need patterns. This variable may also be taken up in future research.

6. In India the industries are in various technological stages, ranging from highly sophisticated and advanced to very punitive and backward industry. It is likely that if we divide these industries in two or three groups, we may obtain different kinds of relationships between job performance and other variables.

7. Industrial workers working in different industrial units producing textile, chemicals, pharmaceuticals, steel rolling mills, machine tools, electronic equipment, heavy machine etc. may also show some interesting results related to their job performance. This needs to be explored in further investigation.

CHAPTER
ELEVEN

Towards Twentyfirst Century

THE NATURE OF WORK and workforce are undergoing more tremendous changes today than anytime in past. We are preparing for the twentyfirst century in a big way. Some of the implications for such an industrial situation, based on what has already been said in this book, are presented here.

When one talks about the job performance of employees, arguments are often given that by the turn of twentyfirst century man will become less important, because machines (computers) perhaps will be doing all production functions. The author feels that only some aspects of jobs may be completely controlled by machines and man will still be the most important component of the work system.

Work should be felt like a play and not a drugery, because every employee spends more than half of his walking time at work. For such a philosophy of job performance, perhaps we need to change the working climate which is encouraging, enthusiastic, which enhances creativity and does not give rise to any kind of stress and strain. In other words we need to appreciate 'the quality of working life' concept and try to improve it. We need to pay more attention to job enrichment strategy. In the next few years, we may observe new work group structure emerging and alternative forms of organisations evolving. Women are taking entry into every occupation, therefore, managers will have to change their stereotyped impressions about them. Sex stereotyping of jobs also will change.

With the information explosion and education, the nature of employees will also drastically change. The crisis of expection may be seen in some cases. As already seen in this study that employees with higher aspirations, and internal locus of causation show better performance.

The incentive component of the reward package is generally designed to be a 'carrot' for higher motivation for job performance. This 'carrot' doesn't seem to work even today. In the future to come, worth of a person has to be recognized first and then perhaps some incentive may be given just for the sake of it.

With highly sophisticated technology perhaps organisational structures and characteristics will also change.

With change in organisational structures, characteristics, technology and design. We perhaps will need better selection strategies so that the right person is selected for the right kind of job.

If managers truely want to improve employee performance, they must pay more attention to motivational processes at work. Sometimes the same motivation strategy may not work for all the employees. Hence, an exercise in the understanding of psychological components may help him in using a contingency strategy. This is all the more important in view of the fact that individual differences across employees, yet another important factor to be understood. For example often we have heard organisations taking decisions on financial rewards, or increase in pay and expecting better performance in return. This factor might have different value for different people. Hence, it doesn't effect the performance. Whereas if overall work environment is improved, if there are challenges, opportunities for growth respect for human dignity, self esteem and creativity, employee job performance would improve. In this context interpersonal relationships in the organisation and qualities of the supervisor in terms of his trustworthiness, sincerity, honesty etc. are equally important. By suggesting this we are not trying to overlook the importance of 'money as a motivator' totally. This has to be combined with other aspects of the system. The value of this research, and a book like this, lies in the fact that it is primarily to sensitize the managers, administrators and researchers to psychological processes at work.

CHAPTER TWELVE

The Summing Up

THE BOOK HAS PRESENTED a number of assumptions, practices, research revelations, interpretations and analyses about employee performance. The ideas presented may be summed up by highlighting the following points.

WORTH OF A PERSON

An organisation employs a worker, the full person, not just his hands or brain or skill. The employee also joins an organisation with some expectations and perhaps job means a way of life to him. Neither the Organisation would like him to be without an activity, nor will the person like to do so. However, what job has been given to him and what he actually does during the working hours may mismatch at times. He may not be the right person for that kind of a job (not so much from technical training or education point of view, but from psychological point of view). He has to be selected and placed at the right point in the organisation. The word 'worth' here is used for explaining the value we place on the accomplishment of a purpose, which, perhaps, is a social judgment about effectiveness of an individual.

Organisational climate is important

The study reveals that some aspects, of organisational climate are important determinants of employee job behaviour. The climate may differ drastically in similar organisations or may be the same in different organisations, perhaps this is because it flows from the basic philosophy of the organisation. This concept includes both, the physical component and the psychological component. In this context it may be interesting to note an observation from Parrow (1967). He says that the variables within one type of organisation may be such that some schools are like prison, some prisons like churches, some churches like factories and some factories are like universities.

Therefore an industrial organisation has to remain an industry—an economically productive organisation. At the same time its human component has to be given due regard. In fact, the organisational climate has to be such, which in philosophy is much broader than the economic objective.

Motivation is both intrinsic and extrinsic

The motivation for better job performance thus has to take the factors internal to the employee and coming from the organisational system. In this context Finch, Jones and Litterer (1976) have observed that the search for answers to motivational problem, is a complex undertaking. People are different, they have different needs, wants, expectations, ambitions etc. They may also change with new experiences. Therefore, use of money or any single strategy is not probably going to work. Thus, individual differences are important, and motivation is a multidimensional, complex concept.

Towards human oriented management which is Indian

Therefore the management philosophy and implementation strategies that we need for years to come have to be humanistic in approach. Moreover, we need to study Indian workers, their values, cultures and background to evolve a managerial style of our own. The values which flow from our family structures, and socialization, process seem, to play an important role. We need to focus more on 'people problem'. Inspite of the fact that there are some common factors in management of human resources across many countries, the author feels we have yet to meet the challenge of Indian Management.

At the end the author is hopeful that every reader would have enjoyed going through this book. Certain concepts, which have been repeated many times in this book, in many ways must have made their impact.

Appendices

APPENDIX A

PARTICULARS OF INDUSTRIES

Industry No.	*Ownership*	*No. of employees*	*Product*
1.	Public Sector	12,000	Turbines, generators, heavy motors etc.
2.	Public Sector	15,000	Generating equipment, transformers switch-gears, traction motors etc.
3.	Private Sector	330	Automotive panel instruments.
4.	Private Sector	130	Gamma globulin, Albumin.
5.	Private Sector	400	Electrical starters, relays, limit switches, thermostat, motor control products.
6.	Private Sector	275	Ayurvedic medicines and toilet products.
7.	Private Sector	160	Brake parts for automobiles, fuel line, industrial hoses.
8.	Private Sector	300	Synthetic and non-synthetic textile.
9.	Private Sector	1,800	Motor cycle, Scooters, Wheel rim, magneto and automobile parts.
10.	Private Sector	100	Industrial process plants.
11.	Private Sector	425	Cycle freewheels.
12.	Private Sector	500	O.F. Moulding Powder, M.F. Moulding Powder, U.F. Resins, Plastic tools and dies.
13.	Private Sector	250	Hydraulic pumps and hydraulic hoses.
14.	Private Sector	1,000	Fans of all types, room coolers, etc.

APPENDIX B

RATING FORM

Dear Manager/Supervisor,

You are requested to give ratings of the following workers of your department regarding four aspects of their performance. The ratings are on 5 point scale ranging from 'Very Good' to 'Very Poor'. Your frank and unbiased opinion will be of great academic value. This information is in no way connected with the prospects of the employees concerned.

Unless sufficient care is taken, such appraisals are likely to have defects of drifting to extremes or central tendency. Therefore, please make sure that you do not tend to mark most of the employees either as 'Very Good', 'Poor', or 'average'. Let your personal relations not prejudice your opinion.

Thank you,

Name of the Worker :

Characteristic to be rated		Very Good	Good	Average	Poor	Very Poor
Productivity	Quality					
	Quantity					
Co-operativeness with fellow workers						
Behaviour with boss and obedience						
Initiative						

Bibliography

A

Adams, J.S. Towards an understanding of inequity, *J. Abnor Soc. Psychol.* 1963, 67, 422-436.

Allen, Luis. A.M. for management : Theory Y updated. Personnel Journal, Dec. 1973.

Allport, G.W., Vernon, P.E. and Lindzey G. Study of values (rev. ed). Boston : Houghton Mifflin, 1951.

Andrisoni, Paul. J. and Gilbert Nestel. Internal-external control as contributor to and outcome of work experience. *J. App. Psychol.* 1976, Vol. 61, No. 1, 156-165.

Argyris, C. The individual and organisation; some problems of mutual adjustment. *Administrative Science Quarterly*, June 1957.

Argyris, C. Personality and organization. New York : Hap 1957.

Argyris, C. *Interpersonal competence and organizational effectiveness.* Homewood III; Dorsey Press, Richard. D. Irwin Inc. 1962.

Argyle, M. Gardner, G. and F. Cioffi, Supervisory methods related to productivity, absenteeism and labour turnover. Human Relations, 1958, 11, 23-40.

Atkinson, J.W. Towards experimental analysis of human motivation in terms of motives, expectancies and incentives. In Atkinson, J.W. (Ed.) Motives in fantacy, action and society, Princeton: Van Nostrand, 1958.

Atkinson, J.W. *An introduction to motivation.* D. Van Nostrand Company, Inc. 1964.

Agrawal K.G. and Sharma B.R. Gratification, meta motivation and Maslow. *Vikalpa* 1977, Vol. 2, No. 4.

B

Bansal M.R. *Correlates of Managerial Effectiveness Ph.D. Thesis* IIT Delhi 1982.

Bakke, E. *Concept of the social organization.* In modern organization theory Ed. M. Haire New York : John Wiley 1959.

Baldwin, A.L. *A cognitive theory of socialization.* In D.A. Goslin (Ed.). Handbook of socialization theory and research. Chicago: Rand Mcnally 1969, 325-346.

Baumgartel, H. and Sobol, R. Background and organizational factors in absenteeism. *Personnel Psychology*, 1959, 12, 431-443.

Bavelas, A. Communication patterns in task oriented groups. *Journal of the Acoustical Society of America*, 1950, 22, 725-730.

Beer, M. *Leadership, employee needs and motivation.* Columbus : Bureau of Business Research. Ohio State 1966.

Bellows, R.M. *Psychology of personnel in business and industry.* 2nd Ed. Prentice Hall Englewood Cliff, New York, 1954.

Billimoria, R.P. *Productivity and Indian worker. Management Perspective*, 1, Oct-Dec., 1960. pp. 32-35.

Blum, Milton L. and James. C. Naylor. *Industrial Psychology : Its Theoretical and Social Foundations.* A Harper International Edition. Harper & Row, 1968.

Bock, R.D. *Multivariate statistical methods in behavioural research.* McGraw Hill Company : New York. 1975.

Bose, K. Organizational Stress and managerial performance : A theoretical conceptualization, Indian Management, 17 (12) 1978.

Bose, S.K. Employee Morale and Supervision. *International Journal of Psychology*. 1955. 30, 117.

Bose, S.K. Leadership and participation; their effect on productivity. *Indian Journal of Psychol.* 32, 1957, 187-190.

Bose, S.K. Psychological Aspects of Plant Personnel. *Education and Psychology*. 3 (3) 1956, pp. 8-17,

Bose, S.K. A psychological approach to productivity movement. *Indian Journal of Psychology*, 33, 1958.

Bhushan Lal, *Factors related to employee performance*. IIT Delhi Ph.D. Thesis 1984.

Bhatt, L.J. Incentives and working class. *Psychological Studies*, Mysore. 7 (2), 1962, 55-61.

Boulding, J. General Systems theory : The skeleton of science. Management Science 2, 3, April 1956, 197-208.

Brayfield, A.H. and Crockett, W.H. Employee attitude and employee performance. *Psychological Bulletin* 1955, 52, 396-424.

Broedling, Laurie, A. Relationship of internal-external control to work motivation and performance in an expectancy model. *Journal of Applied Psychology*, 1975, Vol. 60, No. 1, 65-70.

Burke, R J. "Are Herzberg's Motivators and Hygienes unidimensional ?" *Journal of Applied Psychology*. Vol. 50, 1966, 317-321.

C

Campbell, D.T. and Fiske, D.W. Convergent and discriminatory validation by the multitrait-multimethod Matrix. *Psychological Bulletin*, 1959, 56, 81-105.

Cartwrite, D. Lewinian theory as a contemporary systematic framework. In Koch. S. Psychology : A study of a Science, Vol. 2 1959, New York : McGraw Hill, 7-91.

Cattell, R.B. and Cattell, A.K.S. Handbook for the individual or group culture fair intelligence test. Scale-2. Institute for personality and ability testing, Coronado Drive, III, 1960.

Child, I.L. and Whiting, J.W.M. Determinants of level of aspiration : Evidence from everyday life. *Journal of Abn. Soc. Psychol.* 1949, 44, 303-314.

Choudhury Kamla. Worker participation in production problems. Proceedings of the first management conference. Ahmedabad, *ATIRA* Feb. 1955, 43-46.

Christopher, O. Effect of perceived instrumentality on the relationship between the valence of pay and job performance. *Journal of Social Psychology*, 1976 (Feb.) Vol. 68 (1), 131-132.

Clark, J.V. Motivation in work groups : A tentative view. Human Organization. Vol. 19, 1960, pp. 199-208.

Cofer, C.N. and Appley, M.N. Motivation theory and research. A Wiley International Edition. John Wiley and Sons Inc. 1964.

Cooley, W.W. and Paul. R. Lohnes. Multivariate data analysis. John Wiley & Sons Inc. 1971, New York.

D

Davis, K. Human relations at work. New York : McGraw Hill, 1962.

Dayal, Ishwar and Mirza, S. Saiyadin. Cross Cultural validation of motivation hygiene theory. *Indian Journal of Industrial Relations.* Vol. 6. No. 2, Oct. 1970, 171-183.

Deaus, K. and Emswiller, T. Exploration of successful performance on sex linked tasks, what is skill for male is luck for female. *Journal of Pers. Soc. Psychol.* 1974, 29, 80-85.

Deci, E.L. Intrinsic motivation. Plenum Press. New York : 1975.

Deci, E.L. Notes on the theory and metatheory of intrinsic motivation. Organizational Behaviour and Human Performance Feb. 1976, Vol. 15, No. 1, 130-143.

Directory and who is who of Faridabad industries EMCO Publications, 1972. 58-A, Industrial Area, Faridabad.

Drucker, P.F. The practice of management. William Heinemann Ltd. 1955.

Dugan, R.D. Evaluating territorial sales efforts. *J. App. Psychol.* 1960, 44, 107-110.

Dunnette, M.D., Campbell, J.P. and Hakel, M.D. Factors contributing to job satisfaction and job dissatisfaction in six occupational groups. Organizational Behaviour and Human Performance, Vol. 2, 1967.

Dwivedi, R.S. *Supervisor's Personality and performance*, Somaiya Publications, Bombay 1978.

Dwivedi, R.S. Some correlates of job performance. *Indian Journal of Industrial Relations*, 15, 1980.

E

England G.W. Dhingra O.P. and Agrawal N.C. *The Manager and the Man : A cross cultural study of personal values.* Kent State University Press, 1974.

Evan, M. William. Organization theory structure, systems and environments. Wiley Interscience Publications. John Wiley and Sons Inc. London : 1976.

F

Feather, N.T. The relationship of persistence at a task to expectations of success and achievement related motives. *J. Abnor. Soc. Psychol.* 1961, 63, 552-561.

Feldman, Summers S. and Kiesler S.B. Those who are number two try harder : The effect of sex on attribution of causality. *J. Person Soc. Psychol.* 1974, 30 : 846-55.

Finch, E.F., Jones, H.R. and Litterer, J.A. *Managing for organisational effectiveness : An experimental approach.* McGraw Hill Company Inc. 1976.

Fleishman, E.A. A relationship between incentive, motivation and ability level in psychomotor performance. *J. Exp. Psychol.* 1958 56, 78-81.

Frank, J.D. The influence of level of performance in one task on the level of aspiration in another. *J. Exp. Psychol.* 1935, 18, 159-171.

French, Elizabeth, G. Some characteristics of achievement motivation. *J. Exp. Psychol.* 1955, 50, 232-236.

French, Elizabeth. G. Effects of interaction of achievement motivation and intelligence on problem solving success. *American Psychologist*, 1957, 12, 399-400.

French, Elizabeth. G. Effects of the interaction of motivation and feed back on task performance. In Atkinson J.W. (Ed.) Motives in fantasy, action and society. New York : Van Nostrand 1958, 400-408.

French, J.R.P., Jr., Israel. J., and AS, D. An experiment on participation in a Norwegian factory. *Hum Relat.* 1960, 13, 3-19.

Friedlander, R. and Margulis, N. Multiple impacts of organizational climate and individual value systems upon job satisfaction. *Personnel Psychology*, 1969, 22, 171-183.

Flagnan, J.C. The critical incidence technique. *Psychological Bulletin* 1954, 51, 327-358.

Frieze, I.H. Women's expectations for and causal attribute of success and failure. In social psychological perspective in achievement (Eds.) Madnich Tangri and Hoffman. New York : Holt, Rinehard & Winstin, 1975.

Fruchter, B. *Introduction to factor analysis*. D. Van Nostrand Company Inc. 1954.

G

Gagne, R.M. and Fleishman, E.A. *Psychology and human performance.* A Holt-Dryden Book 1959. Henry Holt and Company, New York.

Ganguly, H.C. An enquiry into incentive for workers in an Engg. Factory. *Indian Journal of Social Work*. 1954, 14 (1) June.

Ganguly, H.C. *Industrial productivity and motivation*. Asia Publishing House. Bombay, New Delhi; 1961.

Ganguly, T. The workers attitude towards the management. *Indian J. of Psychol.* 1953, 28, 29-37.

Galbraith, J.R. and Cummings, L.L. An empirical investigation of the motivational determinants of task performance : Interaction effects between instrumentality—Valence and motivation ability. Organizational behaviour and Human Performance, 1967, 2, 237-257.

Gallerman, S.W. *Motivation and productivity*. American Management Association : Inc, 1963. Indian reprint, D.B. Taraporewala & Sons Pvt. Ltd. 1967.

Georgopoules, B.S., Mahoney, G.M. and Jones. N.W. A pathgoal approach to productivity. *J. Appl. Psychol.* 1957, 41, 345-353.

Ghiselli, E.E. Dimensional problem of criteria. *J. Appl. Psychol.* 1956, 40, 1-4.

Ghiselli, E.E., and M. Haire. The validation of selection tests in the light of the dynamic characters of criterion. *Personnel Psychology*, 1960, 13, 225-231.

Goldman, A.I. *A theory of human action.* Prentice Hall Inc. New Jersy : 1970.

Greene, C.N. *The satisfaction-performance controversy.* Business Horizon. Oct. 1972, 31-41.

Greene, C.N. Causal connections among manager's merit, pay, job satisfaction and performance. *J. Appl. Psychol.* 1973, 58 : 95-100.

Guetzkow, H. and Simon, H.A. The impact of certain communication nets upto organization and performance in task oriented groups. *Management Science*, 1955, 1, 233-250.

Guilford, J.P. *Psychometric Methods.* Tata McGraw Hill Co. Ltd. Bombay-New Delhi 1971.

Guion, R.M. *Personnel testing.* McGraw Hill, New York, 1965.

Gupta, M. A study of job satisfaction among women workers, *Indian Journal of Industrial Relations.* Vol. 14, No. 3, 1977.

Gupta P.K., Pestonjee D.M., and Singh V.S. Worker efficiency in relation to alienation, participation and anxiety. Paper presented at the 20th International Congress of Applied Psychology : Edinburgh, 1982.

H

Hall, D. and Lawler, E. Unused potential in research and development organizations. Research Management, Vol. 12, 1969, 339-54.

Hall, D.T. and Nougaim, K.E. An examination of Maslow's need hierarchy in an organisational setting. Organizational Behaviour and Human Performance, 1968, 3, 12-35.

Harrell, T.W. Differences between men in big and small business. *Personnel Psychology*, 1971, 24, 649-652.

Harris, C.W. *On factors and factor scores.* Psychometrica, Vol. 32, (1967), 363-379.

Hellriegel, D. and John. W. Slocum. Organizational climate : Measures, research and contingencies. *Academy of Management Journal.* Vol. 17 (1974) 255-280.

Herman, J.B., Dunham, R.B. and Hulin, C.L. Organizational structure, demographic characteristics and employee responses. *Organizational Behaviour and Human Performance*, 1975, 13, 206-232.

Hunt, J.K., Hill, J.W. The new look in motivation theory for Organizational Research. *Human Organization.* Summer 1969, 100-109.

Herman, J.B. and Hulin, C.L. Studying organizational attitudes from individual and organizational frames of reference. *Organizational Behaviour and Human Performance*, 1972, 8, 84-108.

Hersey, Paul and K.R. Blanchard. *Management of organizational behaviour : Utilizing human resources.* Prentice Hall of India, New Delhi, 1974.

Herzberg, F.B. Mauser and B.B. Snyderman. *The motivation to work.* New York : Wiley 1959.

Hicks, H.G. and C.R. Gullett. *Organizations : Theory and behaviour.* McGraw Hill 1975.

Hill, J.W. *An application of decision theory to complex industrial behaviour.* Dissertation, Detroet, Wayne State University 1965.

House, W.C. Actual and perceived differences in male and female expectancies and minimal goal levels as a function of competition. *J. of Personality*, 1974, 42, 493-509.

House, R.J. and Wigdor, L.A. Herzberg's dual factor theory of job satisfaction and motivation : A review of evidence and criticism. *Personnel Psychology*, 1967, 20, 369-389.

Hulin, C.L. and Smith, P.A. An empirical investigation of implications of the two factor theory of job satisfaction. *J. Appl. Psychol.* Vol. 51, 1967, pp. 396-402

Hunt, J.M. Motivation inherent in information processing and action. In O.J. Harvey (Ed.) Motivation and Social Interaction New York : Ronald, 1963, 35-94.

Huse, E.F. and Bowditch, J.L. *Behaviour in organization.* Addison Wesley Publishing Company. Inc. Reading, Mass. California, London : 1973.

J

Jalota, S., R.N. Pandey, S.D. Kapoor and R.N. Singh. Socio-economic scale questionnaire (SESSO-Urban) manual. Psychocentre, T. 22. Greenpark. New Delhi-16, 1970.

James, E.V. and Kanungo, R. A study of effective supervision. *Indian Journal of Appl. Psychol* 1966, 3, pp. 1-9.

Jedamus, P., Frame, R. and R. Taylor. Statistical analysis for business decisions. McGraw Hill Book Company Inc. New York. 1976.

Joe, V.C. Review of the internal-external control construct as a personality variable. *Psychological Reports*, 1971, 28, 619-640.

K

Kahn, R.L. Review of F. Herzberg et. al. The motivation to work. *Contemporary Psychology*. 1961, 6, 9.

Kaiser, H. The varimax criterion for analytic rotation in factor analysis. *Psychometrica*, 1958, 23, 187-200.

Kanungo, R.N. Productivity, satisfaction and involvement : Some methodological issues, Paper presented at the 20th International Congress of applied psychology. Edinburgh 1982.

Kast, E.F. and Rosenweig, J.E. *Organization and management : A. system approach*, Second Ed. International Student Edition 1970, McGraw Hill, Inc.

Katzell, R.A. Barrett, R.S. and Parker, T.C. Job satisfaction, job performance and situational characteristics. *A Appl. Psychol.* 1961, 45, 65-72.

Katz, D. and Kahn, R.L. *The social psychology of organizations.* John Willey and Sons. Inc. 1966.

Katz, D., Maccoby, N., Gurin, G. and L.G. Floor. *Productivity, Supervisions and morale among railroad workers.* Ann Arbour. University of Michigan. Survey Research Centre, Institute for Social Research, 1951.

Katz, D. Maccoby, N. and Morse, N.C. *Productivity, supervision and morale in an office situation.* Ann Arbor. University of Michigan. Institute for Social Research, 1950.

Katz, D and Stotlahd, E. "A preliminary statement to a theory of attitude structure and change." In S. Koch (Ed.) Psychology : A study of a science, Vol. 3; Formulations of the person and the social context, New York : McGraw Hill, 1959, 423-475.

Kaufmann, H. Task performance, expected performance and responses to failure as functions of imbalance in the self concept. Doctoral dissertation, Philadelphia, University of Pennsylvania 1962.

Kelly, J. Organizational Behaviour. Home Wood Ill. Irwin, 1969.

Kendal, M.G. *A course in multivariate analysis.* London : Charles Griffin and Co. 1957.

Kirchner, W.K. and M.D. Dunnette. Using critical incidents to measure job proficiency factors. *Personnel*, 1957, 34, 54-59.

Kish, Leslie. *Survey sampling.* John Wiley and Sons Inc. New York : 1965.

Klein, G.S. Need and regulation. In Jones, M.R. (Ed.) Nebraska, Symposium on Motivation, 1954. Lincoln University of Nebraska Press, 224-274.

Knowles, W.H. Human relations in industry : Research and concepts. *California Management Review.* Vol. 1, No. 1, Fall 1958, 87-105.

Koch, S. Behaviour as intrinsically regulated : Work notes towards a pretheory of phenomena called "motivational". Nebraska Symposium on Motivation. 1956, 4, 42-87.

Koch, S. Psychological science vs. the science-humanism antinomy: Intimations of a significant science of man. *American Psychologist*, 1961, 16, 629-639.

Kohn, M.L. and Schooler, C. Occupational experience and psychological functioning : An assessment of reciprocal effects. *American Sociological Review*, 1973, 38, 97-118.

Korman, A.K. Towards an hypothesis of work behaviour. *Journal of Appl. Psychol.* 1970. Vol. 54, No. 1, 31-41.

Kornhauser, A. Psychological studies of employee attitudes. *J. Conslt. Psychol.* Vol. 8, 1944, 137-148.

Krech, D. Crutchfield, R.S. and E.L. Ballachey. *The individual in society.* McGraw Hill, New York : 1962.

Kureshi, A. Personnel appraisal—Problems and issues. In Proceedings of Seminar on Personnel selection and Appraisal System, 1974, pp. 127-131. Organized by Indian Statistical Institute, New Delhi.

L

Lahiri, D.K. and Srivastava, S. Determinants of satisfaction in middle management personnel. *J. Appl. Psychol.* 1967, 51 (3), 254-265.

Lal. M. and Bhardwaj. G. Motivation across three job levels, *Vikalpa*. Vol. 6, No. 2, April, 1981.

Lanham, E. Job evaluation. McGraw Hill Book Company. Inc. New York : 1955.

Lawler, E.E. The multitrait-multirater approach to measuring managerial job performance. *Journal of Applied Psychology*. 1967, 51, 369-381.

Lawler, E.E. III, Motivation in work organizations. Monterey. Calif. Brooks/Cole, 1973.

Lawler, E.E. and Porter, L.W. The effect of performance on job satisfaction. *Industrial Relations*, Vol. 7, No. 1, 1967, 20-28.

Lawrence, L.C. and P.C. Smith. Group decision and employee participation. *J. Appl. Psychol.* 1955, 39, 334-337.

Lazaras, R.S. and Baker, R.W. Personality and psychological stress. A theoretical and methodological framework. *Psychol. Newsletter*, 1956, 8, 21-32.

Leavitt, H.J. *Managerial Psychology*, 2nd Ed. The University of Chicago Press. Chicago, 1964.

Lefcourt, H.M. Internal-external control of reinforcent : A review. *Psychological Bulletin*, 1966, 65, 206-220.

Lefcourt, H.M. *Recent developments in the study of locus of control.* In B.A. Maher (Ed.). Progress in experimental research in personality, Vol. 6, New York : Academic Press, 1972.

Levinson, H. Management by whose objectives? *Harvard Business Review*, July-August, 1970, 125-134.

Levy, Leon H. *Conceptions of personality. Theories and Research.* Random House, Inc. 1970.

Lewin, K. *A dynamic theory of personality.* Selected Papers. New York : McGraw Hill, 1935.

Lewin, K. *The conceptual representation and measurement of Psychological forces*, Durham, N.C. University Press 1938.

Lewin, K. *Field theory in social science*, 1951, New York : Harper.

Lewin, K. Dembo, Tamara, Festinger. L. and Sears, P.S. Level of aspiration. In Hunt, J. Mc V (Ed.) Personality and behaviour disorder 1944. Vol. 1, New York : Ronald Press.

Likert, R. Motivation : The core of management. 1953. in Agrawal (Ed.) *Dynamics of Personnel Management in India.* Tata McGraw Hill Pub. Co., Bombay 1973.

Likert, R. *Motivational approach to management development.* Harvard Business Review 1959, 37, 75-82.

Likert. R. *New patterns of management.* New York, McGraw Hill 1961.

Lindsay, C.A, Marks, E. and L. Gorlow. The Herzberg theory: A critique and reformulation. *J. Appl. Psychol.* 1967. Vol. 51, pp. 330-339.

Littman, R.A. Motives, history and causes. In Jones. M.R. (Ed) Nebraska Symposium on Motivation, 1958. Lincoln : University of Nebraska Press. pp. 114-168.

Locke, E.A. The nature and consequences of job satisfaction. In Handbook of Industrial and Organizational Psychology. (Ed.) M.D. Dunnette. Chicago : Rand McNally, 1974.

M

Mackinney, A.C. The assessment of performance change. An inductive example. *Org. Behaviour and Hum. Perf.* 1967, 2, 56-72.

Maslow, A.H. A theory of human motivation. *Psychological Review,* 1943, Vol. 50, 370-396.

Maslow, A.H. *Motivation and personality.* New York : Harper, 1954.

Maier, N.R.F. *Psychology in industry* (2nd Ed.) Boston, Houghton, Mifflin 1955.

Maier, N.R.F. and Hoffman, L.R. Group decision in England and the United States. *Personnel Psychol.* 1962, 15. 75-87.

Mathur, P. and Sharma. A. 1978. Employee attitude and job performance. An exploratory study in some Indian Industries, *Journal of Engineering Production*, 2, 1978.

Matteson, M.T., J.T. McMohan and Margaret McMohan. Sex differences and job attitudes : Some unexpected findings. *Psychological reports*, 1974, 35, 1333-1334.

Mayo, E. *The human problems of an industrial civilization.* New York : McMillan Company, 1933.

Mc Greger, D. *Human side of enterprise.* New York : McGraw Hill Book Company, 1960.

Mc Keachie, W.J. Motivation, teaching methods and college learning. In M.R. Jones (Ed.) Nebraska symposium on motivation, 1961. Lincoln, University of Nebraska Press 111-142.

Meglino, M.B. A theoretical synthesis of job performance and the evaluating dimensions of organizational climate : A social Psychological perspective. *Academy of Management Review.* July 1976, Vol. 1, No. 3.

Mehta. P. *Motivational approach to organization development,* National Labour Institute Bulletin April, 1978.

Mehta P. *Work motivation in Indian Public Sector. Some conceptualization,* National Labour Institute, Bulletin March, 1978.

Meyer. H.H., Key. E. and French J.R.P. *Split role in performance appraisal.* Harvard Business Review, 1965, 43, 123-129.

Mitchell, F. Motivation to work. In handbook of work, organization and society. (Ed.) R. Dubin, 1976. Rand McNally College Publishing Company, Chicago.

Moon, C.G. and Hariton T. Evaluating an appraisal and feed back training programe. *Personnel,* Nov-Dec., 1958.

Morrisey, L. George. *Appraisal and development through objectives and results,* 1972, Addison-Wesley Publishing Company Inc. Phillipines 1972.

Mukherjee, B.N. Importance of job related needs by Indian textile mill workers. *Indian Journal of Industrial Relations.* Oct. 1968, 4(2), pp. 162-181.

Mukherjee, B.N. Background factors and mass media exposures as predictors of general awareness level among factory workers in five developing countries. In, A Perspective on psychology in India (Ed.) Bimleshwar De and Durga Nand Sinha. Eagle Offset Printers, 15, Thornhill Road, Allahabad, 1977.

Mukherjee, B.N. and Menon, A.S. Personality characteristics and intra-individual variability in industrial output. *Indian Journal of Industrial Relations.* April, 1969 4(4), pp. 462-481.

Mulder, M. Communication structure, decision structure and group performance. *Sociometry,* 1960. 23, 1-14.

Mulder, M. Power equalization through participation? *Ad. Science* Quarterly Vol. 1, March 1971.

Muthayya, B.C. Level of aspiration and intelligence of high achievers and low achievers in the scholastic field. *J. Psychol. Research* 1962. 6, 146-149.

N

Narain. L. *Managerial compensation and motivation in public enterprises*, New Delhi Oxford IBH Publishing Company, 1973.

Newstrom, J.W., William, E. Reif. and Robert, M. Monzeka. Motivating the public employees : Facts vs. Fiction. Public-Personnel Management Jan-Feb., 1976.

Noditch, Murray, P. and Thomas Demaio. Locus of control and competence. *Journal of Personality*. Dec. 1975, Vol. 43, No. 4.

O

Overall, J.E. and Klett, C.J. Applied multivariate analysis. McGraw Hill Company Inc. 1972.

P

Pareek, U. A conceptual model of work motivation. *Indian Journal of Industrial Relations*, 1974, Vol. 10, No. 1.

Parrow, C. A framework for the comparative analysis of organizations. American Sociological Review, 1967, 32.

Peak Helen. Attitude and motivation. In Jones, M.R. (Ed.) Nebraska symposium on motivation, Lincoln : University of Nebraska Press, 1955, 149-188.

Pervin, L.A. Performance and satisfaction as a function of individual-environment fit. *Psychological Bulletin*, 69, 56-58 (1968).

Pestonjee, D.M. and Akhtar, S.S. Occupational values, preference, and income aspiration of engineering and teacher training students. *Indian Psychological Review*, 1969, 5(2), 131-135.

Pestonjee, D.M. and Basu Gopa. A study of job motivation of Indian executives. *Indian J. of Industrial Relations*. 1973, Vol. 8.

Pestonjee D.M. and Y.K. Singh. Performance in relation to anxiety and job envolvement. Paper presented at the 20th international congress of Applied Psychology, 1982.

Porter, L.W. Job attitudes in management I. Perceived deficiencies in need fulfilment as a function of job level. *J. Appl. Psychol.* Vol. 46, No. 6, Dec. 1962. 375-384.

Porter, L.W. Job attitudes in management II : Perceived importance of needs as a function of job level. *J. Appl. Psychol.* Vol. 47, No. 2, 1963, 141-148.

Porter, L.W. Managerial thinking—An international study. New York : Wiley, 1966.

Porter, L.W. and Lawler, E.E. *Managerial attitude and performance* Homewood : III. Irwin, Dorsey : 1968.

R

Rajappa P. Motivation Management. *National Labour Institute Bulletin*, June, 1978.

Rao, Sarweswara, G.V. Theoretical and empirical considerations of the two factor theory of job satisfaction, *Indian Journal of Industrial Relations*. 1972, Jan, Vol. 7(3) 311-330.

Rao, G.V.S. and Rao, V. Ganapathy. A study of factors contributing to satisfaction and importance of Industrial personnel : A test of the two factor theory. *Indian J. of Industrial Relations* 1973, Vol. 9 (2) 233-262.

Rao, T.V. and S.N. Chattopadhyay. A study of the perceptions of organizational climate by employees of Small industries. *Indian J. of Industrial Relations* 1974, Vol. 10, No. 2.

Raush, H.L., Dittman A.T. and T.J. Taylor. Person, setting and change in social interaction. *Human Relations*, 1959, 12, 361-378.

Ravi Kumar R, and K. Harigopal. Managerial job attitudes : Perceived need importance in relation to job level. *Indian Journal of Industrial Relations* 1978, Vol. 13, No. 4.

Reynold, M. Perceptual defence and Herzbergs methodology. A basis for understanding commitment to work. *Interpers. Develop.* 4 : 170-176, (1973-74).

Roth, H.F. Output rates among butter wrappers I, work curves and their stability. *J. Appl. Psychol.* 1946, 30; 199-211.

Roth, H.F. Output rates among butter wrappers II, frequency distributions and a hypothesis regarding the restriction of output. *J. Appl. Psychol.* 1946 (b) 30, 320-327.

Roth, H.F. Output rates among machine operators I, Distributions and their reliabilities. *J. Appl. Psy.* 1947, 31. 384-389.

Roth, H.F. Output among chocolate deppers. *J. Appl. Psychol.* 1951. 35, 94-97.

Roth, H.F. and C.T. Nye. Output rates among coil winders. *J. Appl. Psychol.* 1958, 42, 182-186.

Roth, H.F. and C.T. Nye. Output rates among machine operators II. consistency related to method of pay. *J. Appl. Psychol.* 1959, 43, 417-420.

Roth, H.F. and C.T. Nye. Output rates among machine operators III. A non-incentive situation in two levels of business activity. *J. Appl. Psychol.* 1961, 45, 50-54

Rothlisberger, F. and Dickson, W.J. *Management and the worker.* Cambridge, Mass. Harward, 1939.

Rotter, J.B. The role of the psychological situation in determining the direction of behaviour. In Jones M.R. (Ed.) Nebraska Symposium on motivation. Lincoln : University of Nebraska Press, 1955, 245-268.

Rotter, J.B. Generalized expectancies for internal versus external control of reinforcement. Psychological monographs. *General applied*, Vol 80 No. 1, 1966.

Rotter, J.B. External control and internal control. *Psychology Today*, 1971, 5, 37-59.

Rowe, A.J. Computer stimulation : A solution technique for management problems. Proceedings, Fall joint computer conference, 1965, 27, 254-267.

Ruderman, P. George, Employee merit rating. Handbook of business administration. (Ed.) N.B. Mayard 1967, pp. 144-156.

Rush, H.M.F, The world of work and behavioral sciences : A perspective and an overview. Behavioral Science, Studies in personal Policy No. 216, N.I.C.B. Inc. 1969. in Contemporary Readings in Organizational Behaviour (Ed.) Fred Luthans. McGraw Hill Company. 1972.

S

Saiyadin, Mirza. S. Worker's participation and decision making : Research and hypothesis. *Productivity*, Jan-Mar. 1977, Vol. XVII. No. 4.

Saunders, George B. and John. L. Stanton. Personality and influencing factors in decision making. Organizational behaviour and human performance 1976, 15, 241-256.

Schein, E.H. Organizational psychology. Prentice Hall, Inc., Englewood Cliffs, N.J. 1972.

Schultz, D.G. and A.I. Siegal. The analysis of job. Performance by multidimensional scaling technique. *Journal of Appl. Psychol.* 1964, 48, 329-335.

Scott, W.G. Human relations in management : A behavioral approach. Homewood, III : Irwin, 1962.

Scott, W.E. (Jr.) The effect of extrinsic reward on intrinsic motivation. A critique. Orgn. Behaviour and Hum. Perfor. Vol. 15. No. 1, Feb. 1976.

Seashore, S.E., Indik, B.P. and Georgoloulos, B.S. Relationship among criteria of job performance. *J. Appl. Psychol.* 1960, 44, 195-202

Sequeria, C.E. Characteristics of effective supervisors, Monas, 9 1962, 1-12.

Sikula, Andrew, F. Values and value systems : Importance and relationship to managerial and organizational behaviour. *Journal of Psychol.* 1971, 78, 277-286.

Singh A.P. and Singh B.V. Productivity in relation to ego strength, participation and job anxiety of industrial workers. Paper presented at the 20th International Congress of Applied Psychology. 1982.

Singh A.P. and Singh B.V. Effect of participation and anxiety on performance of blue collar workers. Paper presented at the 20th International Congress of Applied Psychology Edinburgh, 1982.

Singh, T.N. and Baumgartel, H. Background factors in airline mechanics work motivation : A research note. *J. Applied Psychology*. 1966, 50 (5), 357-359.

Sinha, D. Social and behavioural problems in industry. *Indian Journal of Social Work.* 21 (3), 1966, 235-247.

Sinha, D. Review of researches in industrial psychology in India. In A survey of Research in psychology. Sponsored by Indian Council of Social Science Research. New Delhi. Popular Prakashan, Bombay, 1972.

Sinha, J.B.P. Some problems of public sector organizations. National Publishing House, 23, Daryaganj, Delhi, India, 1973.

Sinha, D. and Agrawal, U.N. Job satisfaction and general adjustment of Indian White Collar Workers. *Indian Journal of Industrial Relations,* 1971, 6, 357-367.

Sinha, D. & Nina Gupta. Need satisfaction and absenteeism. *Indian Journal of Industrial Relations,* July. 1974, Vol. 10, No. 1.

Sharma, Anuradha and Mathur P. Unlocking the secret of job performance : A note on value orientation. *Integrated Management,* Vol. XV, Sept. 1980.

Sharma, Anuradha and Mathur P. Poverty: A psychological study. Paper presented at the First annual conference of Social Science Institutions, New Delhi, 1981.

Sharma, Anuradha and Mathur P. Potential Moderator variables in job satisfaction—job performance relationship. Paper presented at the 20th International Congress of Applied Psychology, Edinburgh 1982.

Sharma, Baldev, R. A Review of Researches in India in A survey of Research in Management. Sponsored by Indian Council of Social Science Research, New Delhi 1973. Vikas Publishing House. Delhi, pp. 129-283.

Sharma. B.R. Employee motivation and employer-employee relations in India. *Indian Management,* June, 1983.

Srivastava, A.K. Life Satisfaction of executives, A case study. *Indian Journal of Industrial Relations,* 1978, 14, No. 1.

Shrode, A.W. and Voich, D. (Jr.) Organisation and management—Basic system concepts. Richard, D. Irwin, Inc. Homewood III, 1974.

Spence, J.T. The thematic apperception and attitudes toward achievement in women : A new look at the motive to avoid success and a new method of measurement. *J. Consult. Clin. Psychol*, 1974, 42, 427-437.

Sreeniwasan, K. *Productivity and Social Environment.* Asia Publishing House, Bombay, 1964.

Stagner, R. Perception : *Applied aspects.* In 'the psychology of industrial conflict' John Wiley & Sons Inc. New York : 1956.

Stephen, S.M. Supervisory style and productivity. *Personnel Psychol.* 1966, 19 (3) 275-286.

Sutermeister, R.A. *People and Productivity*. McGraw Hill Company Inc. U.S.A. 1963.

T

Taylor, C.W., W.R. Smith, B. Ghiselin and R. Ellison. Explorations in the measurement and prediction of contributions of one sample of scientists. Personnel Laboratory, Lackland Airforce Base, Texas 1961.

Taylor, D.W. Toward an information processing theory of motivation. Nebraska symposium on Motivation. 1960, 8, 59-79.

Taylor, Ronald, N. Age and experience as determinants of managerial information processing and decision making performance. *Academy of Management Journal.* Vol. 18, No. 1, March 1975, 78-81.

Taylor, W.F. *Scientific Management*, New York : Harper, 1911.

Tiffin, J. Sex merit rating systems. *Personnel Journal*, 1959, 37, 288-292.

Thanga, M.N. *Level of aspiration among factory workers in a telephone factory in India.* Mysore University Ph. D. Thesis, 1959, India.

Tolman, E.C. *Purpose behaviour in Animals and Men.* New York : Century, 1932.

Tolman, E.C. A Psychological Model. In Parsons, T. and Shels, E. (Eds.) *Toward a general theory of action.* Cambridge, Mass : Harvard University Press 279-361.

Tolman, E.C. Principles of purposive behaviour. In S. Koch (Ed.) *Psychology : A study of a science* (Vol. II) New York : McGraw Hill, 1959, pp. 92-157.

Turner. W.W. Dimensions for foreman performance. A factor analysis of criterion measures. *J. of Appl. Psychol.* 1960, 44, 216-223.

U

UNESCO Study. Social and Cultural factors affecting productivity of industrial workers in India. Delhi. UNESCO Research Centre on social and economic development in Southern Asia, 1961, 51.

V

Van Zelst. Sociometrically selected work teams increase production. *Personnel Psychology*. Vol. 5, No. 3. 1952, Automn.

Vernon, P.E. and Allport, G.W. A test for personal values. *J. Abnor. Soc. Psychol.* 1931, 26, 231-248.

Vitles, M.S. *Motivation and morale in industry*. New York : Morton, 1953.

Vroom, V.H. Some personality determinants of the effects of participation. *J. Abnor. Soc. Psychol.* 1959, 59, 322-327.

Vroom, V.H. The effects of attitudes on perception of organizational goals. *Human Relations*, 1960, 13, 229-240.

Vroom, V.H. Ego-involvement, job satisfaction, and job performance. *Personnel Psychology*, 1962. 15, 159-177.

Vroom, V.H. *Work and motivation*. John Wiley & Sons, Inc. New York : 1964.

Vroom, V.H. A comparison of static and dynamic correlation methods in the study of organizations. Organizational behaviour and Human Performance. 1966, 1, 55-70.

W

Wanous, J.P. A causal-correlational analysis of job satisfaction and performance relationship. *J. Applied Psychology*, 1974, 15 : 139-144.

Weiner, B. *Theories of motivation : from mechanism to cognition*, Chicago, Markham, 1972,

Welford, A.T. *Fundamentals of Skill.* Methuen and Co. Ltd. London 1968.

Whisler, T. and Harper, S. *Performance Appraisal : Research and Practice.* Holt, Rinehart & Winston 1962.

Whitla, D.K. and Tirrel J.E. The validity of ratings of several levels of supervisors. *Personnel Psychology*, 1953, Vol. 6, No. 4.

Whyte, F.W. *Money and Motivation*, Harper and Row. Inc., New York : 1955.

Wood, D.A. Background characteristics and work values distinguishing levels among engineers. *Journal of Applied Psychology*, 1971, 55, 537-542.

Wyer, R.S. (Jr.) *Cognitive organization and change : An information processing approach.* Lawrence Erlbaum Associates, Inc., 1974.

Z

Zeleznik, A., Chistensen, C.R. and Rothlisberger, F.J. *The motivation, productivity and satisfaction of workers : a prediction study.* Boston : Harvard University, 1958.

Subject Index